BANKING WITHOUT BOUNDARIES

A History of Security Pacific Bank Washington

BANKING WITHOUT BOUNDARIES

A History of Security Pacific Bank Washington

ROBERT SPECTOR

Documentary Book Publishers Corporation

Bellevue, Washington

Library of Congress Catalog Card Number: 88 - 051549
Library of Congress Cataloging Information:
Publication date: August 1, 1989
Spector, Robert, 1947 -
BANKING WITHOUT BOUNDARIES,
A History of Security Pacific Bank Washington
Bibliography
Includes Index
ISBN 0-935503-06-4
FIRST EDITION

Book and cover design: TeamDesign, Seattle
Printed and bound in the United States of America.

TABLE OF CONTENTS

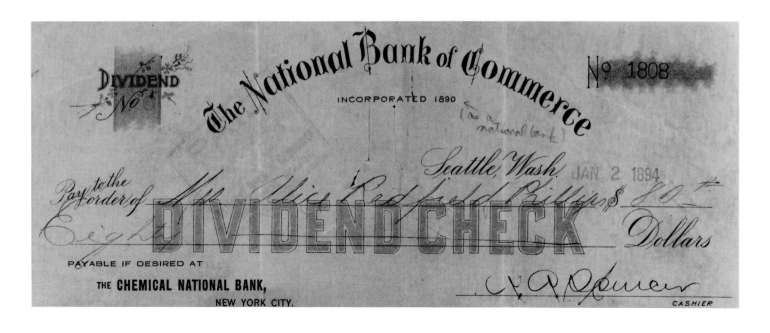

Seattle's pre-fire Front Street (First Avenue) in 1889.

ACKNOWLEDGMENTS

This book is a product of the cooperation, candor and enthusiasm of the men and women who made this organization what it is.

Thanks go to the more than 60 people who were interviewed, several more than once, who offered keen insights into the character of the leaders of NB of C and Rainier Bank years, particularly Maxwell Carlson and G. Robert Truex, Jr.

Unfortunately, Mr. Carlson died before this project began. Bob Truex, although in ill health, participated in two separate interview sessions covering about four hours. Ironically, he died the day this manuscript was submitted to the bank.

Several people were particularly helpful. T. Robert Faragher provided me with personal notes and correspondence covering his tenure as president of the bank. C. Bruce Emry, first vice president and manager of Corporate Communications, encouraged and squired this project from the beginning. Vivienne C. Burke, assistant vice president and manager of the bank's Information Center, opened up the bank's archives to me, pointed me in the right directions and kept me supplied with paper for the copy machine.

Special thanks to Ronald H. Mead, senior vice president and treasurer, and M. Ward Hughes, assistant treasurer and assistant secretary, for their exacting reading of the manuscript and for making sure the numbers added up.

Elliot Marple, the dean of Pacific Northwest business writers, was generous with the notes of his interviews with NB of C and Rainier principals, particularly Maxwell Carlson and Bob Truex. For the complete account of this bank's early history, I recommend *The National Bank of Commerce of Seattle, 1889-1969*, written by Elliot Marple and Bruce H. Olson.

Thanks to Barry Provorse, who filled many roles: publisher, co-interviewer, sounding board, editor and, above all, friend.

Finally, thanks to Marybeth Spector, who possesses the ideal temperament for the wife of a writer.

Robert Spector
Seattle, Washington

(Left) Maxwell Carlson, 1906-1987.
(Right) G. Robert Truex, Jr., 1924-1988.

This book, *Banking Without Boundaries*, commemorates 100 years of Security Pacific Bank Washington accomplishments. Our early history, *The National Bank of Commerce of Seattle*, marked our first 80 years of growth in the Pacific Northwest and highlighted the accomplishments of our distinguished predecessors, Robert Spencer, Manson Backus and Andrew Price.

Over the last four decades, this bank has been dominated by two men, Maxwell Carlson and G. Robert Truex, Jr. This book is dedicated to these two unique individuals.

Their tenures, along with those of Andrew Price, Jr., and T. Robert Faragher, speak volumes of the immense sense of tradition, stability and commitment to this company—a company that it is my distinct honor to lead.

Although quite different in personality and style, Maxwell Carlson and Bob Truex shared a love for, and fascination with, banking. They were men of few hobbies, and banking was both their vocation and avocation.

Mr. Carlson, as we all referred to him, was a prescient man, a student of the industry. He understood the importance of international banking for a retail bank in Seattle. He guided the bank into the electronic age. A reasonable idea that was well-conceived and well-presented would almost certainly gain his ready approval. Most importantly, he established a corporate culture that fostered carefulness, attention to detail, an atmosphere of family and loyalty, and, above all, honesty and integrity. Mr. Carlson died in September 1987.

Bob Truex was an uncommon man. He was an exceptional leader of people, demanding and wise. He set a standard for all those who worked with him as well as for the industry. He struck a good balance between the interests of employees, the company and the community. He did more than direct the bank's cadre of officers; he led by example and encouraged us to follow.

Perhaps Bob's most outstanding characteristic was his concern for people. He was a compassionate human being who was interested in the well-being of everyone in this organization, industry and community.

Bob's death in August 1988 was a great loss for all of us. He left large shoes to fill. As author Robert Spector observed, Bob helped transform this company from one that had become relatively conservative into one that is very progressive, yet carefully managed. Those of us who worked with him carry on that legacy.

We are proud of the history of this organization and excited about our vision of the future for this bank and the Pacific Northwest. As Manson Backus, an early president of NB of C, said: "I have myself carefully watched this big parade of development in the Northwest for nearly 40 years, and I am convinced that all that has been accomplished up to this time is nothing compared to what will be done in the future."

From my perspective, what we have seen is only an indication of what is yet to come. It is our bank's destiny to play a leading role now, and in the future, in the Pacific Northwest.

John D. Mangels
Chairman

Robert R. Spencer (fourth from right) found cramped Front Street office space for the Bank of Commerce in the bookstore of Griffith Davies.

Robert Spencer liked what he saw. Boom-town Seattle in 1888 was all that the lean, mustachioed banker had hoped for on his first visit to the Pacific Northwest. Discouraged by the lack of growth opportunities in his native Iowa City, Iowa, the 34-year-old Spencer was searching for greener pastures, and the brown dust kicked up by the horse-drawn wagons on Commercial Street might have choked his throat, but not his optimism.

The mood was feverish. Wrote Norman H. Clark in *Washington: A Bicentennial History*, "There had been nothing like it in the American history since the opening of the Louisiana Territory—golden years when no personal ambition, however grandiose, seemed at all unreasonable, when it seemed that every venture might prosper and every family might share in the nobility of wealth because of the democracy of profit."

Land prices were spiraling, and the economy was expanding. Seattle, population 43,000, was overtaking rival Tacoma as the Northwest's leading seaport and was

about to gain equal status with the Commencement Bay city as a railroad terminus for James Hill's Great Northern—the second line to link the Pacific Northwest to the rest of America.

The assiduous Spencer approached his trip West with the thoroughness that would become his trademark. Months earlier, he had requested from the postmasters in Spokane Falls and Seattle "the names of some gentlemen of known standing and having the confidence of the citizens and not engaged in the banking business." Later, he queried those businessmen "as to the advisability of starting another bank in your city."

Despite growth in the industry, Spencer had a hunch there was room for one more bank. The city's first, Dexter Horton & Company, had been started in 1870—less than two decades before. By 1880, Washington Territory had one national bank and six private banks. In 1886, the Territory enacted new legislation that eased restrictions on starting new banks. By 1889, the Ter-

Robert R. Spencer, founder of the Bank of Commerce.

1

ritory's 39 national banks accounted for almost $13 million in deposits. Another $5 million was on deposit in the 29 territorial banks, with about $2.35 million of that total in one institution—the Dexter Horton Bank.

Before reaching Seattle, Spencer visited Spokane Falls (later renamed Spokane), the Palouse Valley, Walla Walla, Portland and Tacoma. At each stop, he gathered information on the amount of deposits, the interest paid on time deposits and the profits earned by each bank.

He was most excited about his prospects in Seattle which, along with Tacoma, was replacing Portland as the financial and trade center of the region. In Seattle, forest products, coal, farm crops (particularly hops and wheat) and seafood were gathered, processed, bought and sold, then shipped by rail—via the Northern Pacific, through Tacoma, and later by the Great Northern and Canadian Pacific. These goods would go to the American heartland and, by ship, to San Francisco, then across the sea to foreign ports, mainly to the burgeoning markets of Asia.

Spencer was pleased to find that Seattle's banks had a total of a mere $750,000 in capital, "really not one-half what it would in my judgment support," he wrote. He began raising capital from connections in Washington and Iowa to fund the stock to start a new bank.

The National Bank of Commerce

By January 1889, he had amassed $72,500 in subscriptions. On May 15, he opened the Bank of Commerce on one side of a Front Street (now First Avenue) bookstore owned by Griffith Davies, who became a stockholder and the bank's first depositor. The second deposit was made by G.O. Guy, founder of a drugstore chain that bore his name.

The Bank of Commerce was an almost immediate success, supporting Spencer's belief that he could make a go of it in Seattle. But his confidence soon would be tested. On June 6, a fire started in the basement of a Madison Street wood shop, three blocks north of the bank, and it spread. By the time the fire was contained, it had engulfed 50 blocks of the new city, including most of the business district. Total damage was $15 million, only $3 million of which was insured.

The Bank of Commerce was left with an undamaged safe, but its office was gutted of furniture, fixtures and stationery worth about $2,000. Fortunately, the prudent Spencer had taken out a $1,250 insurance policy the previous week. He quickly hustled up a new space for the bank inside a grocery store on Second and Cherry and was back in business.

The Seattle fire, rather than impeding the city's growth, actually accelerated it. The city regenerated itself like a living organism reproducing tissue. Buildings sprang up all over the city, and construction workers swarmed the city ready to do a job. Local banks were kept busy financing the construction and the small businesses that were popping up, not only in Seattle but throughout the state as well. Washington's population growth rate was 14 times the national rate.

Such grittiness and determination were typical of the people of Seattle. *The Seattle Times* reported: "Everywhere

(Left) Cherry Avenue and Front Street. Shown is all that was left of the bank and the bookstore following the Seattle fire of June 6, 1889.

(Right) A temporary home for the Bank of Commerce was established in a wooden building at the corner of Second and Cherry.

confidence in the future of this city is maintained… The heaviest losers are the most cheerful." Growth could not be reined in, much less stopped. The population grew from 3,533 in 1880 to 43,914 in 1890. Washington had 75,116 people in 1880 as a territory, and 357,232 a decade later, having become a state on November 11, 1889.

In early 1890, Spencer secured a national bank charter and renamed the institution the National Bank of Commerce (NB of C). At the same time, the bank increased its capital from $100,000 to $300,000 through the sale of additional stock, and became one of the state's larger banks.

There was no shortage of competition. From 1888 to 1892, more banks were formed in Seattle than during any time in the city's history. But many of them closed in the aftermath of the economic panic of 1893. Although the nation's economy collapsed, Spencer's prudent business practices kept his bank on a relatively even keel.

Seattle's broad-based economy enabled the region to be less affected by the 1893 panic than many areas of the country; the first Seattle bank did not fail until mid-1895. Washington, although slowed down, continued to build major industries in forest products, agriculture and seafood products—all of which NB of C helped finance. Following the panic, Washington became the nation's largest lumber-producing state, and irrigation created new, productive farmlands in central and eastern Washington.

But the most exciting event was the announcement of the discovery of gold in the Yukon. On July 17, 1897, the steamer *Portland* pulled into Seattle with what somebody claimed was "a ton of gold." Whatever the amount, Seattle tirelessly promoted itself to the rest of the country and very soon established itself as the gateway to Alaska. For Washingtonians, wrote historian Norman H. Clark, "there seemed to be every reason for the faith in a glorious

(Left) Open for business in their first real banking office, Robert Spencer (left) and his brother, Oliver, manned the teller cages at First Avenue and Yesler in 1892.

(Right) Spencer moved his bank uptown in 1897 to a new office at Second Avenue and Cherry.

future" and "to suppose that development and progress would surely go on forever."

Banking Consolidation: Enter Manson Backus

As the region grew, so did financing demands on local banks. Federal law restricted a national bank from lending more than 10 percent of its capital and surplus to any one customer. Consequently, local banks often had to split the business, either with another local bank or with institutions as far east as New York.

Clearly, the fragmentation of the local banking industry impeded the growth of individual institutions, and Spencer and the other bankers realized that the time had come for consolidation. Mergers and acquisitions became the new order of the day. NB of C actively pursued this course of action but was unsuccessful until 1906 when Spencer got together with one of his competitors, Manson F. Backus, the dean of Seattle bankers.

The careers of Backus and Spencer closely paralleled each other. Backus established his operation, Washington National Bank, on July 21, 1889, a mere two months after Spencer opened the Bank of Commerce. Backus had emigrated from upstate New York and, like Spencer, had been lured by the attractions and opportunities of the Pacific Northwest. By 1906, Washington National had $5 million in deposits, about $1 million more than NB of C. Moreover, the diminutive, Napoleonic Backus had earned the respect of his competitors. Years later, Joshua Green of Peoples Bank, referred to his friend Backus as "the keenest, best all-around banker I ever knew."

Prior to meeting with Spencer, Backus had been ruminating over selling his bank because of pressures of increased competition. Nevertheless, the event that pushed him to action was a notice in 1905 by his bank's landlord, the Dexter Horton estate, to vacate the bank premises. Rather than search for new quarters for the bank, Backus decided to explore the possibilities of buying, selling or consolidating. He was contacted by J.W. Maxwell, an NB of C officer, who arranged a meeting with Backus and Spencer on March 14, 1906, at which the two men agreed to merge the institutions. The transaction included an exchange of stock and a sale of additional shares, which raised the total capital to $1 million.

Backus became president, with Spencer and Maxwell as vice presidents. Spencer insisted—and Backus agreed—to retain the name National Bank of Commerce. NB of C, claimed Backus, had the largest deposits "west of Minneapolis in the northern tier of states" and was "in shape to handle any business which is likely to be offered for some years to come."

Backus backed up his boasts with results. Assuming the reins of leadership from Spencer, Backus expanded the bank's loan portfolio, particularly in the state's primary businesses—forest products (mainly logs, lumber and shingles) and salmon-packing. Agriculture had not yet become an important industry to banks west of the Cascade Mountains. The state's leading crop, wheat, was virtually the domain of eastern Washington and was not usually financed by Seattle banks. Gradually, farm production increased in the central and eastern sections of the state as apples, soft fruits and vegetables from Washington became staples in the American home.

All three industries, forestry, fishing and agriculture, were susceptible to the whims of nature and therefore were fraught with risk. But those who could not handle risk could hardly be bankers in the Pacific Northwest. Banking was, inherently, a people business. As NB of C's E.K. Bishop said of the bank's first decade in the 20th century: "Banking depended on the way a lender sized up the borrower. If the banker liked you, he would not even look at your financial statement—if you had one."

The year 1914 was pivotal for the fledgling Washington economy. That year, the opening of the Panama Canal enabled a greater share of lumber from the West Coast to reach the lucrative East Coast markets.

That same year, war broke out in Europe, which created increased demand for products supplied by Seattle industries, particularly ships built on Puget Sound, wood and agriculture products. The increased import-export business helped the Port of Seattle grow to become the

Manson F. Backus.

fourth largest in the country, handling a half-billion dollars worth of goods—one-third more than San Francisco.

The balance sheets of NB of C reflected this boom period. Deposits in 1919 reached $22 million—an 80-percent jump from 1915. In the same period, deposits for all Seattle banks doubled to $186 million.

NB of C rapidly outgrew its headquarters. In 1909, the bank moved from the Bailey Building (later the Second and Cherry Building) to the new Leary Building (later the 1000 Second Avenue Building) at Second and Madison. In 1918, NB of C purchased the Baillargeon Building on Second and Spring, a site where it remained—through renovation and expansion—until the move to the Rainier Bank Tower more than a half-century later.

Despite the success of the bank, Backus and Spencer "did not get along very well," recalled J.A. Swalwell, NB of C's cashier at the time. "Backus had his room on the north side of the bank, Spencer on the south side. I sat in

the middle: I was the go-between." Their personal and philosophical power struggle ended in 1916 with Spencer's death at the age of 61.

Manson F. Backus (second from left) in the bank's customer lobby on the first floor.

Andrew Price

Throughout this period, the canny Backus had looked into numerous acquisitions and mergers but was unable to bring any about. By 1928, Backus, then 75, became a seller, not a buyer.

He could look with pride upon the accomplishments of his 20-year presidency of NB of C: Deposits had tripled, and the bank had reached new heights of size and earnings. Backus liked to point out that an investor who had purchased $100 of Washington National stock 20 years before would have received $5,439 in cash and stock dividends.

NB of C was surely a valuable property. And no one in Seattle was more interested in it than a young man named Andrew Price. Price was bright, imaginative and aggressive, with a confident attitude that rankled the Seattle banking establishment, which associated respectability with advanced age. Price's principal liability—in their eyes—was that he was, by trade, an investor, and not a banker.

After a two-year stint at Yale, Price returned home to Seattle in 1910 to join his father's firm, John E. Price & Co., investment bankers who specialized in underwriting municipal bonds for financing construction of schools, bridges and irrigation systems. The firm also traded bank

Andrew Price as an Army officer in World War I.

stocks and published a quarterly report on every Seattle bank. Young Price had a strong desire to found a bank, using his father's firm and capital as its base. As a first step, he took over a controlling interest in John E. Price & Co. in 1919, and gained working capital from the sale of preferred stock.

Price had surveyed the Seattle banking landscape and knew he had to establish a niche in the marketplace that the other banks were not serving. Aware that the major accounts were firmly entrenched at the established banks, Price opted to become a retail banker, reaching out to the average person who needed a bank to handle his small account.

In the middle of 1919, he opened the Marine State Bank—in the John E. Price offices on Second and Columbia—and promoted the business with a series of newspaper advertisements encouraging savings. One newspaper ad proclaimed: "The man who spends as he goes, goes no farther than spending." After six months in business, Marine was able to boast 460 deposit accounts for a total of $555,633.

Price relished this aggressive approach to business. He was "the darnedest combination of carnival pitchman and conservative Scotsman or banker that you ever saw," recalled Herbert E. Vedder, who would later become the bank's advertising and public relations director. "He could think up more ideas than anyone I ever saw. They were like clay pigeons thrown up in the air. But he had the ability to shoot them down as fast as he threw them up. He would say, 'That's no good.'"

Price was hungry for acquisitions and was determined to establish a branch banking system. He realized early on that the public wanted convenient locations in which to do their banking, just as they preferred buying their groceries near home.

Nevertheless, branch banking had been prohibited by the National Banking Law and, regionally, by a 1909 Washington State banking law that also barred out-of-state banks from doing business in Washington. Only those branches that were the products of Washington State mergers and acquisitions—such as the Dexter Horton Bank—were allowed to continue operation after the law was enacted.

Nationally, branch banking was frustrated through Supreme Court decisions. So Price took a different tack: Rather than have a branch banking system under the umbrella of one bank, he opted to acquire and hold under common ownership the stock of nominally independent banks, which gave them the advantages of expanded resources and economies of scale.

In June 1925, Marine National Company, an invest-

In 1927, Price founded a holding company, Marine Bancorporation, whose capital was used to fund the acquisition of additional banks for the Marine empire.

Price was on a fast track. By the end of 1920, he had converted Marine from a state to a national bank. In 1922, Marine National acquired the deposit liabilities of the failing Northwest Trust and State Bank, which nearly tripled Marine's deposits to almost $5 million. In less than three years of existence, Marine had become the eighth largest of Seattle's 22 commercial banks. Marine had outgrown its offices and moved into the old NB of C building at Second and Madison. That same year, Marine purchased the remains of the failing Scandinavian-American Bank in Ballard for $15,000.

Following the capitalization of Marine National, Price purchased the Capital National Bank of Olympia.

a term that he coined but, later, was unable to register as a trade name.

Generating capital through the sale of non-voting (also called "fully participating") stock, Marine eventually raised $14 million, and Price was ready to acquire new banks. In rapid succession, during the first quarter of 1928, Marine bought the Capital National Bank of Olympia, which was headed by its largest stockholder, C.J. Lord; the National City Bank in Seattle; and the Grays Harbor National Bank in Aberdeen, Washington. The acquisition of the last bank brought to Marine a young officer named Maxwell Carlson, who would eventually become president of NB of C.

The Battle for NB of C

Price was frustrated in his quest for other acquisitions until he turned his attention to NB of C, which had reached $21 million in assets, making it one of the biggest banks in the city. Price met with Backus at the Olympic Hotel, and Backus said he would accept $700 a share for NB of C, which was slightly less than three times the current book value of $250 per share.

ment affiliate of Marine National Bank, purchased King County State Bank, which became Marine State Bank (not to be confused with Price's original Marine State Bank). The following year, he opened a new bank, the Marine Central, on the ground floor of the new Medical and Dental Building near the new downtown retail core. The three banks of the Marine group operated separately, but shared centralized auditing, personnel and other functions. Collectively, the banks had more than 17,000 depositors and resources of around $17 million.

The Marine group's prosperity whetted Price's appetite for expansion throughout Washington. Borrowing a page from the success of the A.P. Giannini holding company, Bancitaly Corp., Price formed a holding company that would acquire his existing banks and was positioned for future bank acquisitions. He dubbed this new organization Marine Bancorporation. "Bancorporation" was

During the 1920s, Federal Reserve Bank members were allowed personalized currency that was secured by government bonds.

First National Bank head M.A. Arnold, however, presented Backus with a counter-proposal that would pave the way for a three-way merger of First National Bank

of Seattle, Metropolitan National and NB of C. Arnold's action set off a bitter fight for the votes of shareholders across the country.

Very soon it became clear that one of the major points of contention in the merger talks was Andrew Price himself. Considered a commercial banking outsider, Price was, in the eyes of the Seattle banking establishment, a "promoter"—of mergers, acquisitions and stock. He had never headed a large institution, and his bancorporation concept was new and untested. No wonder Price would be called by *Fortune* "l'enfant terrible" of Seattle banking.

Nevertheless, after several months of battling, Price —with the backing of Olympia banker Lord and Mark E. Reed, head of Simpson Logging Co. in Shelton—emerged the victor, and consummated the merger with NB of C on May 4, 1928. Backus, 76, remained president of NB of C.

Marine Bancorporation was an immediate success, and in a 1928 message to Marine stockholders Price wrote, "No other Pacific Northwest financial organization has made such progress in such a short time. Its profits, instead of accruing to a small group, are equally divided among over 7,000 stockholders. As the organization is composed of long-established, proven money-making financial institutions, it has been possible to pay dividends during the first year of operation in the aggregate sum of $408,987.07."

Price found this a profitable but divided victory. Soon after the merger, a group of directors and officers departed NB of C to form a new institution, Pacific National Bank, which very quickly built up $6.7 million in deposits, as against NB of C's total of $24.2 million.

In 1929, Arnold engineered the biggest bank merger in the city's history, involving Dexter Horton, First National and Seattle National, which was to become Seattle-First National Bank. With $92 million in deposits, the new bank was almost three times the size of the banks in the Marine group, including its newest acquisitions, the Montesano State Bank, Bank of Elma and First National Bank of Mount Vernon. Seafirst and NB of C would remain first and second in the state for many decades.

Growth was stalled by the stock market crash of 1929 and ensuing Depression. Washington State, so heavily de-

Fortune magazine referred to Andrew Price, young by banking standards, as Seattle's "l'enfant terrible" of banking.

*Marine Bancorporation
stockholders' breakfast,
January 2, 1928.*

pendent on commodities, saw the bottom fall out of the forest products and farm markets. NB of C fared relatively well, dropping only 9 percent in deposits from 1929 to 1932. Overall, Seattle banks slipped 16 percent, and Washington State banks 39 percent. Nationally, under President Franklin D. Roosevelt, the banking system was stabilized by the National Banking Holiday of 1933, which produced a positive psychological effect from the coast-to-coast closing, auditing and subsequent reopening of banks under the close scrutiny of the Comptroller of the Currency. This was followed by the creation of the Federal Deposit Insurance Corporation (FDIC) and the easing of federal laws on branch banking.

Following the reopening of the banks in 1933, Washington State moved toward legalization of branch banking. Price was prepared: He converted most of the remaining Marine banks to NB of C branches and began acquiring institutions east of the Cascade Mountains. In the interim, Backus had been named chairman of the board and Price president.

When Backus died in 1934, J.W. Maxwell became chairman of the board. Maxwell was a longtime advisor to Price and served as a director of both Commerce and Marine Bancorporation from 1928 until his death in 1951.

Washington State limped through the Depression. Unemployment remained high. But out of this period of negative events came positive and evolutionary changes in the foundations underlying the state's economy as it moved from being based almost entirely on natural resources (particularly coal and lumber) to being increas-

ingly dependent on products manufactured from the region's still abundant natural resources. Plentiful, inexpensive hydroelectric power for new heavy industry, such as aluminum smelters, came from federal government-funded Depression-era power projects on the Columbia River at Bonneville and Grand Coulee Dam in central Washington. By the end of the 1930s, these smelters created the aluminum necessary for the increased production of aircraft at The Boeing Airplane Company, which employed more than 6,000 people in 1940 and—spurred on by the war effort—47,000 by 1945. The region also became a major shipbuilding center during World War II.

The forest products business, responding to the dwindling availability of old-growth timber, turned to the manufacture of plywood and the production of pulp, using an abundant supply of forest waste. With pulp readily available, the manufacture of paper products followed.

Agriculture, long a staple of the regional economy, entered a new era thanks to improved irrigation, which added diversity and stability to Washington's crop income. NB of C continued to be a specialist in agricultural lending and eventually grew to be one of the nation's leaders in that field.

Retail Banking

Because the robust post-war economy spawned a community of consumers, retail banking was a logical step for the innovative Price, who believed in bringing banking to the man on the street.

Like his model, Giannini, Price moved out of strictly commercial banking by establishing a retail banking network through an NB of C branch system that had reached more than two dozen cities in western and central Washington. Those branches were set up to offer a variety of consumer services, including savings accounts, consumer instalment loans, residential and commercial mortgage loans, investment banking (including buying and selling government and municipal bonds) and trust work.

Wendell Sizemore, a longtime bank veteran, began a one-man consumer home improvement loan department under the Federal Housing Administration's Title I program. Edgar Ruth was hired in 1942 to set up the instalment loan department—for dealer financing of automobiles, appliances and mobile homes—which proved to be a pivotal ingredient in the NB of C move into retail banking.

Those were heady times for Price and NB of C. Price had built a 25-branch bank that reached $337 million in deposits (excluding the government war-loan account), ranking NB of C second in size in Washington and 42nd in the country.

Because Price and his associates in the community controlled the bank ownership, there were no battles with competing blocks of shareholders. Price had finally gained the respect of the Seattle banking community, which acknowledged that he was not only a canny businessman, but a prudent, if nontraditional, banker as well.

Price was a driving force for the people around him. He regarded it as one of his duties to keep things moving. He kept a keen eye out for new opportunities and constantly directed his officers to pursue promising ideas. "You did a good job," he would say to an employee, with a pat on the back, and follow it with, "What are you going to do today?"

But Price drove no one harder than he drove himself. To him, working seven days a week was the only way to build the kind of bank he wanted. The word "vacation" was absent from his vocabulary.

In February 1946, his wife Virginia finally talked him into taking some time off, since he had not been feeling his usual energetic self. They set sail on a steamer to Victoria, British Columbia, where he suffered a stroke at the Empress Hotel. Although he never lost consciousness, his body was paralyzed. Andrew Price was now faced with the biggest challenge of his life.

Rest and rehabilitation took the remainder of 1946. By early 1947, Price returned to the bank. But he was a different man. His right arm had no feeling and hung, uselessly, at his side. His speech was slurred—almost unintelligible—and his walk was halting.

Leadership of Marine and NB of C had become uncertain. While he was undergoing his rehabilitation, Price had placed in charge Carl L. Phillips, who had been a vice president. A quartet of bank elders and directors—Ira W. Bedle, Homer L. Boyd, A.W. Faragher and Herbert Witherspoon—were selected as senior vice presidents.

These were merely stopgap measures. Finally, Price reluctantly realized that he could no longer preside over the modern bank that was his creation. Who could replace him? The four bank elders were too old and two of them, Bedle and Witherspoon, had been ill themselves. Price's son, Andrew, Jr., educated as an engineer, not a banker, was only 22 at the time and in military service. Many people felt Phillips, who had been ostensibly managing the bank after Price's stroke, might have been the odds-on choice.

But Price had other ideas. He remained chairman of the board of the bank. Keith G. Fisken, a lumberman and a director of NB of C since 1928, was named president of Marine. Price had no doubt whom his successor should be, but he did go to his old friend and colleague, Marine Director Boyd, for ratification. The man they selected might have surprised some outsiders, but not any one who knew the inner workings of NB of C. In January 1948, it was Maxwell Carlson who became president of NB of C and, at age 42, one of the youngest bank presidents in America. The selection of Carlson, whom Price trusted to protect his family's interests (in tandem with Fisken), was one of the most important decisions Price ever made.

CHAPTER TWO

The Modern Era

Andrew Price (left) and his successor, Maxwell Carlson, following Carlson's election as president in January 1948.

Who's Max Carlson?" wondered some members of the Seattle banking community. Few knew Maxwell Carlson well, and only M.A. Arnold and Frank Jerome of Seattle-First called to congratulate him.

Carlson was born and raised in Aberdeen, Washington, in Grays Harbor County, the heart of the state's verdant timber region. His father, Gust A. Carlson, a Swedish immigrant, became a successful log exporter and was a director of Grays Harbor National Bank. The young, introspective Maxwell was a self-described "bookworm" who, even as a child, enjoyed reading *Barron's*. He was often ill with the lingering effects of scarlet fever and heart problems and later, in college, a duodenal ulcer. Max sometimes confided to friends that he felt he was "living on borrowed time." Despite his health problems, he graduated cum laude from Dartmouth College with a bachelor's of commercial sciences degree in 1928 and gained a master's degree from the Amos Tuck School of Administration and Finance.

Investment banking held an allure for Carlson and, before his senior year in college, his father gave him $10,000 to invest, which Carlson used to acquire bonds. That summer, he worked at the Grays Harbor National Bank, which Marine Bancorporation had acquired in 1928. Following graduation, Carlson returned to join the bank full time as a $60-a-month clerk.

"Actually, I wanted to go into the investment business," he once said. "But all they wanted when I got out of college were salesmen, and I wanted to be an analyst. So I took the best thing I could get, which was a job as a clerk."

In 1930, a year after the stock market crash, which devastated Aberdeen because of the fall in demand for forest products, Carlson moved to Seattle as an assistant auditor on branch examinations. He also gained experience auditing the foreign department, bond accounts and currency, and the trust department. In 1938, Andrew Price named Carlson manager of the Credit Department and, in 1946, operating vice president and assistant loan supervisor.

Clearly, Carlson had reached the inner circle, in which he had become a confidant of Price. In fact, Price sometimes drove Carlson home (they both lived on Capitol Hill) so they could discuss bank business, from loans to personnel promotions. (Carlson made it a practice to interview personally all returning servicemen and new employees, particularly anyone who was felt to have potential above the clerical level.) Price sometimes took the longest way home and the two men would continue the conversation sitting in the car in front of Carlson's home.

Carlson's close communication with Price served him well after Carlson was elected president. Price tried to preside at board and officer meetings, but his speech—as a result of his stroke—was difficult to understand. The frustrated Price might interrupt proceedings by waving a piece of paper in the air, and Carlson somehow interpreted what Price wanted to say. Price would nod or shake his head depending on whether he agreed or disagreed with what was going on. Price began to concentrate his efforts on the bank's public relations and advertising. A natural-born promoter, he had always had a flair for public rela-

(From left)
Maxwell Carlson, Doris A. Hagen, Andrew Price, Carl L. Phillips, A.W. Faragher, Lorraine Myers and Anne Kerbaugh prepare, in 1949, to celebrate NB of C's 60th anniversary.

tions. Inspired by the Coca-Cola logo, Price designed NB of C's logo of a rolling silver dollar. (Although his health never improved, his interest in the bank continued until his death in February 1955.)

Unbeknownst to Price and the other officers, Carlson himself was feeling ill. A workaholic out of the Price school, Carlson generally worked 18-hour days, hadn't taken a vacation since the early 1930s and, at the time he assumed the presidency, was fighting his own battles against fatigue and weight loss. The latter was particularly worrisome because the 6'4" Carlson was naturally reed-thin and had few extra pounds to lose. Finally, at Director Homer L. Boyd's insistence, Carlson spent a couple of weeks in Tucson, Arizona. He didn't take another vacation until 1959 when he attended an international banking conference in Geneva, Switzerland.

Carlson and Price faced pressure from bank executives and stockholders. Some board members wanted Price to relinquish his share in the control of the bank because they feared for its future. Some key people either retired or left, including Carl L. Phillips, who had been passed over for the presidency. The directors' insistence eased only after Carlson proved that the fu-

ture of the bank would be secure in his hands. It would be close to another quarter-century before Carlson's authority would be questioned again.

The Carlson Touch

The success of both nations and companies often rests on being led by the right man at the right time. Price was the right man to create the modern bank for the era between the world wars. Carlson fulfilled the same role for the post-World War II era, which redefined retail banking for a society that became mobile and consumer-oriented; commercial banking for a Washington State business economy that was diversifying into new enterprises; and international banking that established the foundation for the interrelated world economy of the latter part of the 20th century.

Carlson believed that these postwar changes would accelerate with the retirement of bankers who came out of the Depression with a "defensive attitude," as he told business writer Elliot Marple in an interview. Carlson felt that, after the Depression, it was necessary to replace a generation of regulatory officials, bankers and politicians

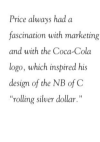

Price always had a fascination with marketing and with the Coca-Cola logo, which inspired his design of the NB of C "rolling silver dollar."

Maxwell Carlson (right) and Randall Marney at the Quincy opening in 1950.

"before you could shake off what the Depression had done. People with a defensive attitude are not aggressive," he felt, in pursuing, accepting and implementing new ideas. During World War II, Carlson said, "bankers moved sideways."

As the older generation of bankers began to retire, Carlson's mark began to appear on virtually every aspect of NB of C. He reviewed the salaries of every bank officer, which were traditionally lower than those of the competition. Nothing escaped his notice. Eschewing an office of his own, Carlson kept his desk out on the third floor facing the other bank officers, in the manner of a school-teacher facing his students. He preferred to roam through the bank and sit down to talk with a man, rather than call him to his own desk. He rarely made idle conversation or spoke to the officers unless he was concerned about a particular subject. "He wouldn't interfere with your operation at all," remembered Chester C. Macneill, who, at the time, was instalment loan manager. "If he didn't talk to you, you knew you were doing a good job."

One of his favorite comments was "I don't promise you anything but opportunity and good intentions."

Carlson "wasn't the kind of man who was disturbed if you had an idea with which he didn't agree," recalled Clarence L. Hulford, retired executive vice president of the International Department. "He didn't object if you brought it back in a different form."

Carlson's work habits were legendary: seven days a week, including Christmas and New Year's Day. Typically, he arrived at the bank at 8:15 in the morning with a large briefcase bulging with homework from the night before. At 5:30, he'd head for home—stopping to quip with chief auditor Harold Fenno, "I'm on my second shift," loaded down with reports, credit files on upcoming major loans and personnel files. A voracious reader, Carlson read up to a dozen newspapers a day. He enjoyed clipping out articles on banking and other subjects related to individual employees' interests and hobbies, according to his secretary, Lenore Petrich. She was assigned to circulate the articles from the "Carlson clipping service."

Carlson was a keen student of economics and business. At board and management meetings, he would predict where interest rates would be six months down the road and would earmark up-and-coming industries in which the bank should be lending money.

Expansion: Branch and International Banking

Carlson's vision for the future of the bank took two distinct tacks: international operations, which dated back to 1908, when Manson Backus made his first trip to Japan, and expansion of branch banking.

Prior to World War II, the bank's "foreign" department dealt mainly with overseas remittances (usually by immigrants), and letters of credit for imports and exports. The end of the war in Europe brought about increased demand for remittances from local residents who had been cut off from their European relatives for six years. After V-J Day, the Philippines and China were reopened to trade, which accelerated so quickly the tiny NB of C

The National Bank of Commerce hosted the governor's luncheon in 1954 on the occasion of the Seattle Trade Fair. Seated at the table are Washington State Governor Arthur B. Langlie (third from left), Maxwell Carlson (fourth from left), Wendell Sizemore (at head of table), Clarence L. Hulford (fifth from right), and Walter F. Clift (far right).

Clarence L. Hulford at the 1954 Seattle Trade Fair.

was the first Seattle bank to establish relationships with Japan after World War II. The Mediterranean, Carlson often said, was "the ocean of the past, the Atlantic the ocean of the present and the Pacific the ocean of the future." He once told a gathering of customers that his father, a lumber exporter, used to tell him, "Max, when the Orient buys lumber from us, we are prosperous. When they do not buy, the Atlantic Coast and Pacific Coast trade cannot make up for it." And, Carlson added: "I have never forgotten that."

In 1949, to head the International Department, Carlson selected Clarence L. Hulford, who had joined the bank two years before, after working with Northwest Airlines. Following a six-month international banking training program at Wells Fargo Bank in San Francisco, Hulford joined a Seattle Chamber of Commerce-sponsored trade trip to Japan in January 1950—one of the first such trips by a chamber group. Privately, Hulford also toured the Philippines, Hong Kong and Thailand.

In the 1950s, Seattle business interests sponsored a series of trade fairs, which included the leading Asian economies, as a means of teaching those countries how to merchandise their products for the American market. (The first Toyota ever seen in the United States was shown at one of those trade fairs.) Financing from the International Department helped step up Far East imports to the Pacific Coast and Washington exports to the Orient.

Because the underdeveloped countries were short of capital, NB of C and other banks devised ways to finance such things as exports of Washington State farm equip-

foreign department was overwhelmed. Louie Delorie, who headed the department, found himself at the bank on New Year's Day of 1947 trying to keep up with the year-end load. At 10 o'clock that morning, Carlson arrived and, in Delorie's words, "blew his top" at the volume of work given one man, and promised him some assistance.

In 1947, the Allies moved to stimulate the post-war world economy. The $12 billion Marshall Plan to rehabilitate Europe was unveiled, the International Monetary Fund was created and the World Bank was set up to extend long-term loans.

Carlson pushed for reestablishing and strengthening the kind of trade relationship that the Pacific Northwest had enjoyed with the Orient before the war, and he was determined that NB of C would be an important player. It ment. The foreign customer would arrange for a loan through his local overseas bank and the correspondent bank paid the Washington manufacturer the moment the equipment was shipped. The customer then used the equipment to generate enough capital to pay back the loan in instalments. This method was especially effective in the Philippines, where Washington logging equipment helped rejuvenate the industry.

Unlike money-center banks, which participated in a wide variety of projects, NB of C concentrated on business that related to Pacific Northwest industry. For example, the bank helped establish the credits that the Japanese Kawasaki company needed to become a manufacturer of helicopter parts for Vertol, a division of The Boeing Company. In forest products, NB of C was one of the principal banks for financing Japanese acquisition of lumber and pulp products from Alaska. To assist the state's agricultural industry the bank financed red beans grown in eastern Washington for key markets in several Caribbean countries. Darigold used NB of C when the dairy company was establishing its first operation in the Philippines. NB of C also helped arrange trade/barter transactions among Asian countries when post-war cash was in short supply.

By 1962, NB of C had developed a sufficient business base and credit volume to establish an office in Hong Kong, but it was opened as a separate corporation, International Bank of Commerce, to protect NB of C's assets. This was typical of the caution exercised by Carlson while in the pursuit of new markets.

Bank of America was the only American bank that preceded NB of C into Hong Kong. The colonial banking authorities had established a short period of time in which they would allow a new bank to be chartered. NB of C remained one of the few American banks permitted to open Edge Act offices in Hong Kong for a long time thereafter. Hulford and Carlson had foreseen this opportunity and had cultivated the image of the bank as being responsible and aware of not only the business opportunities, but also the intricacies of operating in a society so deeply concerned with tradition, solidity and character.

The NB of C office in Hong Kong was permitted to branch bank as any native Hong Kong bank could. As a result, the bank was able to build a deposit base from local businesses and individuals which, as with branches in Washington, in effect paid the administrative costs of the Hong Kong offices. Later, many American banks that set up in Hong Kong were faced with substantial overhead costs and could trade with only the international business they might be able to squeeze away from somebody else.

NB of C added several other branches in Asia and then opened a London branch in 1968—the second West Coast bank to set up operations in London to serve client needs in Europe and the Middle East. The London branch was added to complement the East Asian-Hong Kong development and to provide flexibility in international financing through direct access to the increasingly important market for "Eurodollars"—deposits denominated in U.S. dollars.

The bank's grand plan was to be in at least three major world capital markets: New York, London and

Tokyo, the last added in 1969. The bank's foreign currency exchange traders became essential cogs in the international operation. "Part of our commitment to our clients overseas was to have a source of funds on which we could also depend," recalled Hulford. The transfusion of Eurodollars greatly enhanced NB of C's flexibility both internationally and domestically. By 1969, NB of C deposits in London topped $100 million.

That year, the bank formed an Edge Act corporation in New York City, known as the National Bank of Commerce of Seattle (International). That location better

enabled the bank to serve customer interests in Mexico and Central and South America.

The bank took the initiative in asking the Washington State legislature for an alien banking law that would allow banks domiciled outside the United States to establish branches in the state of Washington. NB of C officers felt that Japanese trading companies would direct more business to the ports of Puget Sound if they had Japanese banks in Puget Sound. They were proved right. Alien bank branches enhanced Washington State's attractiveness for direct trade and commerce.

Branch Banking

The go-go post-war years were highlighted by a nationwide surge in branch banking. The McFadden Act of 1927, and its revision in 1933, had broadened the ability of national banks to increase their branch banking activities, and state banking laws permitted the federal revision. The total number of banks nationwide actually dropped from 15,000 in 1933 to 14,000 in 1950. Yet the number of branches increased from 3,000 in 1933 to 4,100 in 1945 to almost 5,000 in 1950. The number doubled in the 1960s and doubled again in 1970 to almost 22,000.

As a consequence of post-Depression conservative lending and investment methods and a wartime economic boom, banks were sailing on a sea of liquidity, including Treasury securities. They were ready and anxious to extend credit to satisfy pent-up consumer demand for such goods as automobiles, appliances and television sets. At

Seattle's port trade was cyclical, but by the 1960s it was a dominant Seattle employer and business.

NB of C made its first acquisition east of the Cascade Mountains in 1935 when it purchased Yakima First National Bank.

After a long string of eastern Washington acquisitions, NB of C purchased Quincy Valley State Bank in 1950.

the same time, businesses were ready to retool for peace-time expansion.

Seattle's economy mirrored that of the rest of the country. Although, immediately after the war, there were drops in shipping, in lumber exports and in employment at Boeing, the area began an impressive economic buildup in the ensuing decade. According to the book *Seattle, Past to Present*, by Roger Sale, King County in 1947 had 54,000 employed workers responsible for $265 million in value-added products. By 1954, the county had 78,000 workers adding $520 million. "In 15 years [after 1939, the last Depression year] the number of workers had tripled, the value added by manufacture had jumped 600 percent," wrote Sale.

Statewide, the aluminum industry became important, with plants in Spokane, Vancouver and Ferndale; and the nationwide housing boom animated the state's forest products businesses, including pulp and paper.

Locally, real estate and home building also boomed in the post-war era, as Seattle spilled over into the suburbs—where the bank had yet to establish branches. Carlson believed the only way NB of C could grow in Washington was to acquire banks in good locations, and he hired a professor from the University of Washington to study potential areas of growth where NB of C could either acquire an existing bank or build a new branch.

In the 1950s, most of the banks acquired by NB of C were in rural areas. As he did with every other aspect of the bank, Carlson became personally involved with each purchase. If a potential new acquisition was in a farming area, he would consult Walter J. Funk, the bank's agricultural expert, about the value of such a move.

A typical acquisition in those days was a small bank founded and run by one man now on the eve of his retirement. The founder usually was most interested in cashing out his bank's stock interests, which generally represented most of his net worth. Cash transactions best suited Marine Bancorporation, which had little stock to trade. Furthermore, non-voting stock was not attractive to these retiring banking entrepreneurs.

The 1960s marked the era when branch banking became an important tool within the banking industry. Branch banking achieved a higher level of efficiency by way of improvements in electronic communications, data and check processing and electronic funds transfer. Banks invested in the bricks and mortar required to build new branches; the majority of these were *de novo*—new offices—built in the suburbs.

Washington bank law permitted a bank to establish branches only in the city of its principal place of business, in unincorporated areas within that county and in incorporated towns elsewhere in the state that did not already have the services of a commercial bank. Thus, the only way a branch could be established in a city like Bellevue, where NB of C was not represented, was to open a branch in the county on unincorporated land adjacent to the city.

(Left) Goldendale branch, opened June 1, 1948.

(Center) Almira branch, opened July 10, 1948.

(Right) Auburn branch, opened February 14, 1950.

Following city annexation of the property, the branch could be moved to a downtown location. NB of C worked hard to get adjoining property owners to agree that if NB of C talked the city into an annexation vote, they would vote for it. The Bellevue branch was an example of such a strategy.

Carlson oversaw the branch site selections and the building design, and he handpicked branch managers.

NB of C's burgeoning branch system merely extended his network of influence. He liked to refer to the branch managers as his "boys," and promoted a close-knit relationship not only between the head office and the branches, but also among the branches themselves. Even when the number of branches reached 100 around the state, Carlson knew everyone's name, as well as his strong points and weaknesses. He didn't hesitate to call anyone at any time of the day or night to ask him to get on a particular project. Because he often called on branches without notice, his "boys" kept on their toes.

Carlson retained a family-like, paternalistic approach toward running the bank. His attitude was: "If you do your job, don't worry. You'll be treated fairly and everything will be taken care of." An officer who made an error in judgment was rarely fired. Instead, a place for him was found in the bank in which he would be allowed to serve out his time in some make-busy job until retirement.

In those days, when the bulk of the business consisted of taking deposits and making loans, a branch manager in a big office might be in the same job for 10 or 12 years and given a lot of authority. Managers felt that each office was,

in effect, an individual bank that served the entire needs of its community.

John D. Mangels, who worked at the University branch in 1950, recalled: "The manager of that office was NB of C in his community. He was, in effect, the president of that bank. Anything that was needed in the way of banking services, be it automobile loan, home mortgage or trust services, was offered through the branch. Theoretically, every lending officer had the authority to commit the full legal lending limit of the bank to a customer. There were a few who did that—but you had better be right!"

Small Business Administration Loans

In 1961, Carlson believed NB of C should broaden the bank's involvement with small businesses. He brought in Robert F. Buck, a former Seattle regional administrator and later deputy administrator in Washington, D.C., for the Small Business Administration, to broaden the bank's appeal to the middle market. Carlson "was 20 years ahead of his time," Buck recalled. Buck eventually brought in Mangels from the bank's Main Office to help assist branch managers in setting up and servicing SBA loans, which were 85-percent guaranteed by the federal government. Most of these loans could not qualify as a direct bank term loan for such reasons as insufficient working capital, inadequate net worth, lack of collateral or inexperience.

His assignment from Carlson was to "grow customers," Buck recounted. "One of the ways you grow custom-

(Left) Robert F. Buck was hired in 1961 as NB of C's small-business lender. He was assigned by Maxwell Carlson to "grow customers."

(Center) During the early 1960s, Maxwell Carlson directed the bank's efforts toward becoming a larger agricultural lender.

(Right) Since its pioneer days, Washington State has been a major U.S. wheat producer.

ers is to make a bet on their future. One of the ways to make a bet on their future is to become involved in their business by providing term financing which, in those days, was a relatively new thing and was not prevalent in most of the banks around the United States."

One of those companies was Intermec, which today makes bar code equipment that is the standard of the industry and is being used all over the world.

NB of C became the premier SBA lender in Washington and still ranks in the top 10 nationally in dollar volume of SBA guaranteed loans. In doing so, the bank has helped small businesses expand, increased employment and added deposits to the bank's totals.

Branch banks were on the front line of lending for Washington State's most important businesses: agriculture, commercial fishing and forest products.

Agriculture represented 7 percent of NB of C's loan portfolio—more than twice that of most regional banks. At the end of 1963, Carlson wanted to put greater emphasis on this business, which included agricultural production loans to farmers and agribusiness loans to such related companies as food processors. He directed NB of C to carry a separate total for agricultural loans outside the commercial loan portfolio, an unusual practice. In that year, he asked Robert H. Matthews to come to Seattle, to be vice president in charge of the bank's agriculture loan business.

NB of C developed specialty branches for agricultural loans in areas such as Quincy, Moses Lake, Tri-Cities, Yakima, Wenatchee, Mt. Vernon, Burlington and Lynden. "Once you get a good reputation among farmers and businessmen in farm communities, they come to you," noted Matthews. "We're now banking the sons of a lot of the farmers whom we first banked. I'm sure we'll be banking the sons' sons in a few more years."

In commercial fishing loans, NB of C's strongest branches were in the Columbia River area, Grays Harbor, Bellingham and La Conner. But most of the larger loans were in Seattle, where Alaska firms were headquartered.

In forest products, branches in Aberdeen, White Salmon and Longview helped make NB of C one of the country's leading lenders in the industry.

Carlson's Advisors

Executive Vice President Ralph J. Stowell.

In the 1960s, ultimate responsibility for all loans over $50,000 belonged to the Senior Loan Committee, which consisted of the chairman, who was the senior loan officer, and all the heads of divisions: commercial, instalment, agriculture, real estate and control—the nucleus of the bank. The committee dated back to the Manson Backus era and was continued through Andrew Price's regime.

Regarding the Senior Loan Committee, Mangels recalled, "In all my years, I cannot remember an instance when a reasonable

idea that was well-conceived and well-presented did not get approval."

From 1950 through 1966, the chairman of the Senior Loan Committee was the senior loan officer, Ralph J. Stowell, who rose through the bank to become an executive vice president and a director. Stowell was a no-frills, straightforward banker, who combined sound banking practices with good instincts to become one of the most respected credit men in the country.

Stowell, who joined the bank in 1927, developed as a stabilizing force within the company and a close confidant of Carlson, particularly in the latter years of the Carlson era. Mangels described Stowell as "an important force, my mentor. A lot of my business philosophy came out of the Senior Loan Committee structure."

Besides Stowell, Carlson's inner circle included lumberman Keith G. Fisken, who first became a director of NB of C in 1928 and of Marine in 1951, and then served as president of Marine Bancorporation from 1955 to 1962, representing the controlling family stockholders. Another valued advisor was Evan S. McCord, Jr., a senior partner in the corporation's law firm—Kerr, McCord (now Graham & Dunn)—and the son and namesake of a longtime director. The junior McCord also directed the affairs of Pacific American Fisheries, which was once the world's largest salmon canner.

Andrew Price, Jr., joined the bank in 1947 starting as a trainee at NB of C's University branch. He worked in myriad departments and positions, and he was elected its chairman in 1965. He began representing the Price family interest on Marine's board in 1953, eventually becoming its president in 1962 and its chairman a decade later.

Carlson ran a very conservative, tightly controlled—and profitable—ship. "Liquidity," he would often say, "is an important word as long as I am around the bank. The important thing is to maintain the quality of assets so that in adversity you can rely on yourself." To that sentiment, he added one of his favorite mottos: "The time to be careful is when everything seems wonderful."

In those days, banks could manage earnings in a singular manner, and Carlson made sure NB of C's assets were clean and sound. Consequently, he would write off bad loans much sooner than other bankers. Any loan that was classified as "doubtful" would soon be written off, so every loan looked good. Although the "doubtful" loans went off the books, the bank would still try to collect on them. The recovery rate was always good because many of the questioned loans turned out, with time, to be good assets for the bank. Carlson recognized that loss charges

against earnings were a means to manage earnings. His objective was to have the bank's earnings grow at a rate of 10 percent each year.

John Hall, an executive vice president of Marine, a director of NB of C, and once a partner in the law firm of McCord, Moen, Sayre, Hall & Rolfe, recalled: "For instance, in a very good year, in order to bring earnings down to the 10-percent level, [Carlson] would put money into the pension fund. And in a year that was going to be tougher, he'd keep sending the budget back to the various department heads to rework until it showed a 10-percent improvement in earnings. It never varied much. But that was consistent with his philosophy of being a kind of

Evan S. McCord, Jr.

With caution, Maxwell Carlson (left) and Robert C. Cummings introduced NB of C's BankAmericard credit card in 1966.

caretaker [for the Price family interests]."

Hall noted that Carlson was aware of "hidden assets in the bank that, if brought forth, could result in much higher earnings than he was willing to show with his concept of managing those earnings." One such hidden asset was over-funding the retirement plan, so that "in a poor year, you don't have to put as much into it."

Price, Jr., believed that family control of the bank put less pressure on Carlson to be market-sensitive. "There were practically no corporate owners of the voting stock… It was a unique kind of arrangement and I think Max always felt grateful for it. It gave him the opportunity to build soundly without making compromises based on some concern about the market price of a more widely held Marine Bancorporation stock…

"Mr. Carlson often said he did not want to be the one to introduce untried, expensive changes in the bank," Price recalled. Quite often, that philosophy kept the bank out of serious trouble. Other times, it kept NB of C, temporarily, behind the competition.

On the other hand, in 1966 NB of C became one of the first franchisees outside of California for Bank of America's BankAmericard program, which was introduced in 1959. T. Robert Faragher was given the overall responsibility for the operation and he tapped Robert C. Cummings and Dee W. Hock to manage it. The only other Washington bank involved with BankAmericard was Puget Sound National Bank of Tacoma. Cummings ran the credit card operation for several years after Hock left the bank to become president of National BankAmeri-

card, Inc. (now VISA) in San Francisco.

Carlson began to ease his stance on borrowing money. The bank made it a policy never to borrow from the Federal Reserve. Even during the Depression, the liquidity-strained NB of C refused to sell preferred stock to the Reconstruction Finance Corporation. But, in 1968, Carlson announced that the bank could not get along without borrowed money: "We're a billion dollar bank; we might as well get the expertise of liability money management." He hoped the bank would never have to borrow from the Federal Reserve and be subject to their regulations. NB of C did, however, borrow federal funds, and also bought some European funds, which were expeditiously returned.

Stock Reorganization

In 1967, attorneys for New York's Citibank discovered a loophole in the 1956 Bank Holding Company Act, which sharply regulated all holding companies owning or controlling two or more banks. One of the provisions of the law required those corporations to divest themselves of non-banking subsidiaries. On the other hand, said the Citibank attorneys, the law did not apply to holding companies owning or controlling only one bank.

Consequently, many banking corporations became one-bank holding companies *a la* Marine, which, thanks to the prescience of Price, Sr., was decades ahead of its time. In 1970, Congress would close some of the loopholes, but it still allowed bank holding companies to diversify into new businesses judged "closely related" to banking; it also allowed these non-banking affiliates to conduct business anywhere in the country, which was the opening step toward interstate banking.

Marine's two-class stock ownership became an anachronism amidst the increase in one-bank holding companies that were formed to take advantage of these loopholes and created, as modern law required, with only one class of stock—all voting. The initial stock, which had the vote, was always sold at a premium over the non-voting shares. The market—such as it was—for Marine stock recognized the value of the voting right. The non-voting shares, however, always sold at a discount from book value. This situation, referred to as the "holding company discount," was common to many companies of similar structure.

Investors and analysts would not touch the stock because they could not acquire voting rights. Insurance companies and other institutional buyers would not put any Marine stock in their portfolios because most state insurance laws precluded purchase of non-voting stock.

Over the years, other companies of Marine's vintage had modernized their structure by converting their two classes of stock to a single all-voting class of stock. Various formulas had been developed, which always resulted in a premium being paid to voting shareholders for their willingness to give up exclusive voting rights. In the early days of Marine, the two classes of stock had traded at about the same price, but in the years prior to 1970, the voting shares had begun to command a substantial premium over the non-voting shares.

Price, Jr., recalled: "It was time to change the structure to do as other companies had done. It was clear that the capital of the company could no longer grow fast enough to meet the bank's opportunities. To market shares in the future required that the non-voting class of shares be made voting. A study was made to determine what might best be done."

On January 28, 1969, at a special meeting of shareholders called by the Marine directors, the new plan for one class of common, voting stock was approved. Ten new voting shares were issued for each of the 352,806 shares of "fully participating" stock. Of that total, 344,966 were owned by approximately 4,100 stockholders, and the remainder held in Marine's treasury. Also, 30 new voting shares were issued for each of the 7,881 shares of "initial" stock held by the Price family and their close associates. The shareholders authorized the issuance of up to a total of 10,000,000 shares of common stock and 500,000 shares of preferred stock for corporate purposes.

The new corporate structure also made Marine's charter from the State of Washington—which was scheduled to expire in 1977—perpetual. At the time Marine was formed in 1927, 50 years was the maximum charter life that the state could grant.

The corporation used its new shares in a tax-free exchange for the net assets of the State Bank of Wilbur.

That same year, Marine acquired Coast Mortgage and Investment Company, the largest mortgage banking company in the Northwest, with a half-billion dollars in its mortgage servicing portfolio. The first major non-bank acquisition following the reorganization, the firm's name was later shortened to Coast Mortgage Company.

The stock conversion was a turning point. As Price wrote in the 1969 annual report: "The corporate life of the Bancorporation is now perpetual, which encourages long-range thinking, planning and action."

Carlson had built NB of C into a solid, if not spectacular, institution. Overall, from 1949 to 1969, total deposits tripled from $344 million to $1 billion, making it the 42nd largest bank in the country. The number of branches grew from 27 to 102, including six in the Far East and one in London. During his tenure, the bank added data processing, municipal bonds, a stepped-up trust department and credit cards, and continued a record of uninterrupted quarterly dividends that began in February 1928.

Succession

Everyone agreed that Carlson would be a hard act to follow. He himself began considering that eventuality in 1965 when he announced to the board that he would retire on December 1, 1970. He later told Elliot Marple that he didn't think that "the old man should hang on indefinitely

T. Robert Faragher.

while able, younger men chafe at the chance to step up." He planned to spend the next five years building an in-depth organization and he wanted to leave a strong force for his successor, rather than problems that should have been handled earlier.

That was easier said than done. In the latter years of his administration, Carlson began to constrict his decision-making circle as several key people began to retire. Among bank officers, Stowell was the only one left who had not been hired by Carlson himself and who could be treated somewhat as an equal.

Carlson would seek out and consider the opinions of others, particularly Stowell. But, Stowell recalled, Carlson worked closer to the vest than anyone he had ever come in contact with. Carlson continued to work day and night and Stowell often told him, "Max, you know very well when you retire it will take two men to take your place."

The bank's board of directors was also experiencing a gradual, inevitable changing of the guard. In 1966, the by-laws had been amended to provide a retirement age of 72 for directors (later it was changed to 70).

The board began actively thinking about Carlson's replacement in 1968 when a number of new people in their 40s joined the ranks, particularly W.J. "Jerry" Pennington, publisher of *The Seattle Times*, and Thomas E. Bolger, president of Pacific Northwest Bell Telephone Company.

"Those people brought a sense of change and accelerated the need to take a look at the bank and its future," recalled board member James A. Walsh, president of Allied Stores. "One of the great concerns of the board was that Max wouldn't delegate authority. You just couldn't have that army of employees reporting to one or two individuals. It made the bank less competitive. It all added up to the fact that Seattle was growing from a town to a major city. We had to respond to that."

In 1965, Carlson tapped Faragher, a senior vice president of the Bank of California, to become an executive vice president of NB of C, one of the few times he hired a senior executive from outside the bank. In fact, when Faragher asked about NB of C's policy on paying moving expenses, Carlson responded that he didn't recollect "what we have done in the past because we hire so few people from the outside."

Yet, Faragher was no stranger to NB of C. His father, Arthur W. Faragher, who had retired in 1953, had been a longtime officer and later vice chairman of the bank, and young Bob used to work summers at Central branch. In 1935, after graduating from the University of Washington with a major in commercial banking, he took a job with Guaranty Trust Company of New York, where he stayed for a year. He returned to the Puget Sound area and was with Peoples National Bank for 15 years, working in the head office and branches as a manager and loan officer, and in time rising to vice president. He later moved to the Bank of California, for which he worked in Tacoma until 1962, when he was promoted to senior vice president and transferred to the bank's headquarters in San Francisco, where he was involved with branch administration.

Although Faragher was brought in as Carlson's heir apparent to become the next president of the bank, initially he had few specific duties. He did some work with the branches, both domestic and international, BankAmericard and bank expansion, as well as civic activities, including chairmanship of the United Good Neighbor campaign. Later, as Carlson decided to explore the building of a new office, Faragher headed that program.

Faragher succeeded Carlson as president of the bank following the annual meeting on January 28, 1971. At the meeting of Marine Bancorporation, Carlson was elected chairman of the board.

Faragher's ascension was part of a larger master plan for NB of C and Marine. A few months earlier, the directors of both entities had approved the signing of an agreement with the directors of Washington Trust Bank of Spokane to merge the two institutions. Carlson had long sought to establish an NB of C presence in what was then Washington's second largest city. Washington Trust, established in 1902, had eight offices in eastern Washington and had deposits in 1970 of more than $87 million. The acquisition involved the exchange of 800,000 shares of Marine Bancorporation stock.

Marine's plan was that it was buying not only a bank, but also a new chief executive and successor to Carlson at Marine—Philip H. Stanton, whose family founded and

but not particularly innovative or aggressive.

Faragher was faced with an economic hurricane. Interest rates, especially short-term, were as volatile as at any time in economic history. President Richard Nixon introduced a three-month wage/price freeze to stem inflation. Money-market yields declined abruptly, business recovery was slow, demand from short-term borrowers was weak, and the international balance of payments was unfavorable. And Seattle, the bank's principal market, was in the throes of a crash.

Internationally, it was a year of successive monetary crises. Domestic interest rates forced European countries to either float or revalue currencies. In August, President Nixon suspended the gold convertibility of the dollar and imposed a 10-percent surcharge on imports in an attempt to force a realignment of exchange rates and the removal of discriminatory restrictions against U.S. imports.

Locally, Seattle was reeling from problems at The Boeing Company because of a decline in airline orders, a reduction in government business and cancellation of the company's supersonic transport program. Shipyards were

controlled Washington Trust. The plan was for Faragher to move up to be chairman of the bank and Stanton to become president. Stanton would succeed Faragher when Faragher retired in six years.

With this scheme set in motion, and with the two parties confident and hopeful that the merger would be approved by the end of 1971, the Faragher era began—but with Carlson's fingers still on the strings as chairman of Marine. Price, Jr., was president of Marine and a director of both the bank and the holding company.

Faragher inherited a bank that most observers— inside and outside the bank—felt was strong and sound, also hurt by a decline in government business, and other key industries mirrored the general downturn in the U.S. economy, including housing and forest products.

Despite Seattle's high unemployment, all was not bleak. The Port of Seattle experienced record export volume, retail sales were strong and downtown construction was booming.

NB of C's performance reflected this mixed picture. The bank achieved its highest net income in history, but net operating income was slightly less than in the previous year. Such a condition was endemic throughout the country in 1971, when major banks increased net operating earnings by an average of only 1 percent over 1970.

In September 1971, the Comptroller of the Currency approved the Washington Trust merger. Nonetheless, the Justice Department filed suit to enjoin the merger, alleging a possible adverse effect on banking competition in Spokane. Because NB of C was not represented in Spokane, state law forbade NB of C from entering Spokane, except through the acquisition of an existing bank.

Emotionally and economically, 1972 was a most difficult year for the bank. The Seattle area was still in the throes of the Boeing bust, but the economy began to rebound in the latter half of the year. Boeing began hiring again, reaching about 42,500 full-time employees, up from around 30,000. Overall, Seattle-area employment reached 559,400 in July, the highest level since the boom year of 1968. Nevertheless, the unemployment rate still hovered at about 9 percent.

Earnings failed to reach the near-record highs of

T. Robert Faragher (left) and Clarence L. Hulford (second from left) greeted guests at the Tokyo National Bank of Commerce office.

1971. Net operating income after adjustments was $8,728,753 compared with $9,549,761, a decrease of $821,008, or 8.6 percent.

The biggest factor in the decline of earnings was the large gain in time deposits, which resulted in a markedly higher cost of funds. At a time when the prime rate reached its lowest point since 1960, NB of C maintained its regular annual passbook savings rate of 4-1/2 percent, while other leading commercial banks cut their rate in April to 4 percent, where it stayed for the rest of the year. In the short term, that policy depressed NB of C's earnings, but in a longer perspective, it probably helped the bank retain and expand its customer base.

Loan losses, particularly in the International Divi-

sion, became another area of concern. The average return on loans dipped below 1970 levels. "The department was faced," recalled Mangels, "with people problems, system problems and credit problems." Carlson made his dissatisfaction well known. Speaking at a board of directors meeting on October 26, 1972, Carlson said, "It took us 20 years… to progress from crawling to walking in international banking. The speed limit has been out of control for some time, and currently, we are far from ready to run in this highly competitive, specialized business."

Faragher moved to select Mangels, then vice president and chairman of the international section of the Senior Loan Committee, to become administrative and credit officer of international banking at the senior vice president level. Faragher told the board that neither he nor Mangels expected the international post to be permanent, "although I believe it will be a very valuable experience in the career of a man who will be an important senior officer in our bank in the future."

Faragher, Mangels and Hulford were eventually able to straighten out the personnel and administrative problems of the division and to recover almost all of the international loans that had been charged off by the bank. By 1974, international loan recoveries exceeded total charge-offs for that year.

Such matters of substance, as well as matters of style, caused a rapidly widening rift between Faragher and Carlson. "Mister" Carlson, of the old school, was formal in his manner and his aloofness came from being shy. "Bob" Faragher was collegial and informal and felt that, in

his way, he was fostering a team approach to banking. He spent his first year treading lightly, yet carefully making subtle changes, such as decentralizing some decision-making responsibilities away from the president's office. But he was keenly aware that he was operating in a bank that was still dominated by Carlson, staffed by people Carlson hired, and overseen by a board of directors Carlson had handpicked.

The situation came to a head at the annual meeting for the 1972 fiscal year, which took place on March 27, 1973. Annual meetings are rarely the site for drama, but this one was an exception. Carlson, the final speaker, publicly expressed disappointment that the bank's performance had interrupted a long history of earnings gains.

"Now is the time to be more demanding," he said. adding that it was important to begin seeing evidence of a turnaround. Ironically, he felt the company needed greater "depth and breadth" of management—the very management he had selected. Unless improved performance was forthcoming from the bank, and the other Marine subsidiaries, he indicated, changes would be made. "Time is of the essence," he concluded.

Perhaps, as some people thought, Carlson was berating not only management, but himself as well. His comments took on an ironic twist in the light of the opening paragraph of his president's report in the 1972 annual report. After announcing the publication of Elliot Marple's history of NB of C, he wrote, "Someday a sequel to the history will reflect that the years 1971, 1972 and 1973 represented a period of transition from one generation of management and control to another, with growing emphasis on professionalism and on responsiveness to public ownership."

Part of that management was Price, Jr., who also served as a balancing force between Carlson, the board and Faragher. If Carlson represented the heart of the bank, Price, Jr., symbolized its soul. A man of estimable character and ethics, Price supported Faragher in the wake of Carlson's criticisms within the board room. As an officer of the corporation, he had a better feeling for the situation than most directors and was willing to put himself on the line. He combined a Jimmy Stewart-like shyness with a sense of fairness to become a valuable member of the corporation in difficult times.

Another asset was Stowell, who had retired as executive vice president of the bank in 1972. He had the trust of Carlson and the respect of the board, and he was asked to stay on as a director. He worked closely with management and interpreted for the board the problems faced by NB of C and the banking industry.

In the meantime, personnel changes at the highest level continued on hold as NB of C waited, impatiently, for the resolution of the Washington Trust merger, which the Justice Department continued to oppose.

With Carlson reaching the age of 67, it became clear that a successor needed to be named. Initially, that was going to be Stanton, but the merger delay created too much paralysis and uncertainty, and Stanton lost some of his enthusiasm for the job.

Carlson appointed his trusted colleague, Stowell, to chair a committee to select Carlson's replacement.

"We needed a chief executive for Marine because under it would come everything outside the bank," recalled Stowell. "At the time, we thought that maybe we could have a head for the corporation and a head for the bank. But I for one never thought it would work. I didn't believe the corporation could own the bank stock and be subservient to the head of the bank. Then we found it was not easy to find a man who would meet our requirements."

It took Stowell and his committee almost a year to find that man.

T. Robert Faragher (right)
and Andrew Price, Jr.,
directed the bank's destiny
through the tumultuous early
1970s.

Marine Bancorporation 1969 board of directors (from left): Maxwell Carlson, Glenn Carrington, Keith G. Fisken, Frank R. Kitchell, Ralph J. Stowell, W.J. Pennington, Andrew Price, Jr., Dean H. Eastman, T. Robert Faragher, A.W. Faragher, Prentice Bloedel, John F. Hall and Wylie Hemphill, shortly after A.W. Faragher's retirement.

G. Robert Truex, Jr., liked what he saw. The view of Seattle from Lake Washington, aboard Winston D. Brown's 45-foot Tollycraft, the *Ann Dee*, was breathtaking. It was a clear, sunny Pacific Northwest day that featured snow-capped Mt. Rainier out in all its glory, the kind of day hoped for by the bank's directors, some of whom— Brown, W. J. Pennington, Louis Arrigoni, Prentice Bloedel and Ralph J. Stowell—also were on board. Truex was the man they were looking for. The question was: Would he take the job?

Stowell and T. Robert Faragher had worked for six months to get Truex to come up to Seattle from San Francisco, where he was a highly regarded executive vice president of the Bank of America— although recently he had been passed over in favor of B of A insider A.W. "Tom" Clausen for the presidency, the highest post in the organization. Because he didn't want to lead the board on, Truex had graciously declined previous invitations; he simply was not interested in the job, he explained. Why did he eventually acquiesce? Years later, when recalling his reasons, Truex quipped, "It was either out of curiosity or just to get them to leave me alone."

Maxwell Carlson, when told of the search committee's interest in Truex, laughed at the absurdity of the idea: "You think you're going to get an executive vice president of B of A to come out to a little regional bank? You're wasting your time."

That sentiment was typical among bankers both in Seattle and around the country. Truex, age 50, tall, good looking, blond hair streaked with gray, impeccably dressed, a senior level executive at the biggest bank in the country, was too sophisticated, too New York and Los Angeles, to be interested in coming to Seattle.

Bob Truex

Truex was born in 1924 in Red Bank, New Jersey, near the Atlantic Ocean, where his ancestors first arrived three centuries earlier. A good student and athlete, Truex, his 1942 high school yearbook prophesied, would find fame as first baseman for the New York Yankees. Instead, he soon found himself not on the ball field, but the battlefield in World War II, serving in four major campaigns with the field artillery as a tank commander under General George S. Patton in the European Theater. Following the war, he entered Rutgers University in New Brunswick, New Jersey, and graduated in 1949 with a bachelor's degree in economics. After interviews with several companies in several businesses, he joined Irving Trust Company in New

G. Robert Truex, Jr.

*G. Robert Truex, Jr.,
(front, second from right)
had his first command as
R.O.T.C. company
commander at Rutgers. In
World War II
he served under General
George S. Patton as a tank
commander.*

For a time, G. Robert
Truex, Jr., served as Bank of
America's deputy executive
of the Southern Division.
His responsibilities included
representing the bank's
support of the Pasadena Rose
Parade. He is shown with
Bob Hope, holding up a
sketch of
B of A's float.

Trained in wholesale banking, he was on the fast track at Irving, becoming a senior vice president at 34 with responsibilities for the National Division. But by the time he reached 40, he felt his "learning curve had flattened out." He had grown weary of the 110-mile-a-day round-trip commutes between Red Bank and New York and the time away from his family; continuing the same routine for the next 25 years was anathema to his thinking.

Truex's hopes and dreams lay far beyond the New York metropolitan area. He felt the lure of the West, where he had traveled extensively for Irving, including trips to Seattle for correspondent business with NB of C. Like Carlson, he believed the future of the country was on the Pacific Coast. He would later explain in an interview with *The New York Times*: "The West, I thought, was a better place to live, more open and dynamic. That's where I wanted to raise my two children."

In 1966, at 42, he took a cut in pay and rank, and left the wholesale business of Irving to join the quintessential retail bank, B of A, as a vice president in charge of international banking, with 100-plus branches overseas. He became a senior vice president two years later and an executive vice president the year after that. He was part of the trust investment policy committee, deputy executive of the bank's Southern Division (covering much of B of A's domestic business), and chairman of the Southern

York City to learn the business of banking.

Why banking and why Irving? Truex described his reasoning to author Brad Williams in *The Anatomy of an Airline, a History of National Airlines*: "I liked the people I met [at Irving] and I thought frankly that the opportunities were greater in the commercial banking business because they didn't have a lot of guys like me pushing to get to the top spots in them. [There were only three men in his trainee class.] It was the lowest financial offer I had, but it was the one I took."

California loan committee, handling two-thirds of B of A's total loan portfolio. He described his B of A experience as "a graduate course in a different kind of banking. I was running great numbers of people, locations and transactions and learned to make decisions regarding large masses of people. I learned about consumer banking and management, and I learned about the West and the Pacific."

In 1971, an entirely different challenge arose in the aftermath of the bombing by a couple of thousand Vietnam War protesters of a B of A branch at Isla Vista, near the campus of the University of California at Santa Barbara. The protesters hurled Molotov cocktails at the branch, setting it on fire because they believed B of A branches held U.S. military funds. And, as a student leader would later explain, the bank was "the symbol of the American dollar." Dozens of branch bombings followed.

Truex recalled: "I kept trying to persuade my colleagues to listen to the students instead of just being incensed, which I was. Nobody wants to see his property damaged wantonly, but let's hear what they've got to say and see if we can't communicate." Truex was named chairman of social policy, a position that B of A management felt had to be filled by a senior officer with credibility. He met frequently with a variety of groups—students, blacks, Chicanos—and initiated bank-sponsored social programs in minority employment, job enrichment and sexual equality.

After Clausen was named president, Truex began receiving job feelers from other banks, including NB of C. Nevertheless, he recalled, "I didn't want to move my

family again, or to leave San Francisco."

Sizing Up the Job

As Truex, his wife Nancy and the NB of C directors skimmed the steel-blue waters of Lake Washington, the view of Seattle—both literal and metaphorical—was bright and abundant. The skyline was being reshaped as the city continued its recovery from the infamous "Boeing Bust" period when the giant airplane maker reduced its Seattle-area payroll by 64,000 over three years. But in the summer of 1973, unemployment had halved down to 7 percent, the Port of Seattle was setting new tonnage records, and the city was in the midst of one of the biggest downtown building booms in the country.

Beginning in 1970, $72 million worth of office buildings, hotels and apartments were built downtown, and another $86 million worth were under construction in the summer of 1973. A total of $200 million worth of private construction projects and $195 million in city projects were either planned or under construction. They included the $25 million, 42-story Bank of California Center; the $17 million, 30-story Financial Center; the $11.5 million, 21-story Peoples National Bank Building; the $38 million, 33-story Pacific Northwest Bell Building; the $60 million King County Multipurpose Dome Stadium; and what was then called "Commerce House," a proposed $35 million, 40-story tower that would be the new home of NB of C.

The view of NB of C was, if not exciting, just as full of promise. The bank and the holding company were rock solid—"a miniature Bank of America," said Truex. "It had a strong retail base, agriculture business, urban branches, international offices and the diversification that goes with them." Marine ranked 89th nationally in earnings and 51st in assets, and those assets were sound. But the company wasn't as profitable as it should have been. It was not geared for marketing—neither of its stock to the investment community nor of its services to consumers. From the stock reorganization in 1969 through 1972, Marine's earnings per share had risen less than 1/2 cent; return on average assets had declined from 0.71 percent to 0.50 percent, compared with an industry average of 0.80 percent.

Truex was intrigued. He had, by his own admission, spent most of his life training to be a chief executive officer. He thought: "Wouldn't it be fun to see if I could get this place moving?" And as he later said in a *Seattle Post-Intelligencer* interview, his wife Nancy "wanted to see me take a shot at it. She thought I would be happier running my own show."

A new era officially began on September 1, 1973, when Truex became president and chief executive officer of Marine. Faragher remained president and chief executive of the bank. In order to make room, Price moved over to become vice chairman of Marine Bancorporation. Price said he felt he "was a member of a team that was in transition…I was strongly in favor of Truex's coming on… Some ground had to give, and I was happy to give there."

Within a year, Truex and Faragher, by mutual agreement, would switch titles. Faragher recalled: "From our first conversation, Bob and I agreed that the principal officers of the holding company and the bank ought to be the same for legal, administrative and operating reasons. A single head for both would eliminate confusion and clarify our organizational structure."

Truex found an institution involved in every conceivable aspect of banking—but doing it inefficiently. There was no formal organizational chart; everyone, essentially, reported to Carlson. There was a lack of communication among the bank's 27 departments in 20 different locations. Residential real estate loans were still being processed by hand, and the bank was not channeling mortgage loans through its sister, Coast Mortgage Company. The loan portfolio included a large proportion of low-yield loans, especially real estate loans. The stock was undervalued. There was a large spread between Seafirst and NB of C on return on equity and assets.

The branch banking system was too centralized—many routine decisions were made in Seattle. One executive estimated that only 25 of NB of C's 110 branches earned a proper return. Furthermore, NB of C had no branch penetration in three important markets in Washington: Everett, Tacoma and Spokane.

Pay and compensation trailed that of other banks (Carlson's salary was twice that of the next closest officer, Stowell), which led to personnel trained by NB of C being siphoned off by other banks.

But the positives outweighed the negatives. Truex told *The New York Times* that NB of C offered "a splendid franchise with a good reputation for soundness, good asset

(Left) In 1964, NB of C
opened its first international
subsidiary in Hong Kong, the
International Bank of
Commerce.

(Right) In April 1968,
NB of C opened an office in
London.

quality and some very good people." The International Department was the equal of any non-money center bank in the country. The bank had one of the nation's best BankAmericard performances. Assets were clean: NB of C had avoided heavy investment in three areas that had caused other banks major problems in the early 1970s—oil tanker loans, New York City issues and Real Estate Investment Trusts (REITs). Truex immediately ordered an increase in lending rates, which he felt were at an unreasonably low level.

The 1973 performance was a vindication for Faragher. NB of C produced a stunning turnaround despite wide fluctuations in interest rates (the prime rate changed 17 times during the year), the high cost of money (an all-time high of 10 percent) and high operating costs. At year-end, resources exceeded $2 billion for the first time in the bank's history. Net operating income jumped nearly 33 percent over the previous year to almost $11.6 million.

The loan portfolio topped $1 billion for the first time and the bank reached an all-time high of 69 percent domestic-loan-to-deposit ratio. The trust portfolio's common fund outperformed the Standard and Poor's 500 Index by 65 percent. Nationally, the bank's stock fund was in the top 10th percentile.

On the personnel side, when Faragher joined NB of C in June 1965, the bank had only two senior officers above the rank of vice president. By mid-June of 1973, there were 11. By year-end, the average age of NB of C branch managers was the youngest in the bank's history.

At the beginning of the 1970s, the employment of women and minority officers increased significantly through the bank's recruiting efforts. In 1970, NB of C assigned its first female branch manager, T. Melvine Verzani, to the Madison Park office.

In 1973, the bank consummated the largest merger in its history when it acquired five branches of the Citizens

State Bank of Puyallup, which was delayed almost two years because of the Washington Trust Bank litigation. It also added three *de novo* branch offices.

NB of C added an Asset and Liability Management Committee, under John D. Mangels, for allocating assets and funding sources.

Despite considerable progress by the end of 1973, Marine shareholders were unhappy with the market price of their stock. Consequently, Truex—whose top priority was creating the greatest value for shareholders—directed his remarks in that year's annual report to them. Marine, he stressed, was "a property that is potentially worth much more than the value currently accorded it in the market-place. As the manager of your investment, I pledge to you an all-out effort toward the objective of achieving for all of us as shareholders the maximum attainable long-range growth of earnings."

He added: "If we were operating at the same level of

profitability as the nation's more successful one-bank holding companies, we would have produced about one-third more of net operating income in 1973. It will take at least a few years to reach that point…"

During the meeting, in answer to a stockholder's question, he made clear management's dissatisfaction with the price of the stock. At the end of 1973, the stock, which would split on two subsequent occasions, had a book value of more than $31 per share, yet a share's quoted market value ranged between $26.50 and $18.50 throughout the year. The day before the annual meeting, it traded at $24.25, prompting Truex to observe: "I'm being paid an outlandish amount to do something about that."

Part of the problem was that Marine stock tended to be closely held and too lightly traded to affect the price. The name itself was another problem. Some potential investors looked for the stock under "NB of C." Some confused the bancorporation with other banks having "Marine" in their name.

The company had hired a corporate identity consultant, Lippincott & Margulies, to study the name and identification. Without indicating what the name change might be, Truex warned the shareholders: "It takes a steel spine to change your name."

Truex reiterated the theme of change whenever and wherever possible—in memos, meetings, speeches and interviews. In the annual report, he wrote that success would be determined by "the capacity of the 3,762 people in all of Marine's units to absorb change." A typical memo of that era: "…change has become a way of life; it is and

In 1970, T. Melvine Verzani of NB of C's Madison Park office, shown with the principals of a local mortgage company, became the bank's first female branch manager.

will remain a constant… we all must be prepared not only to accept change and to manage it, but also to develop a working climate that is conducive to it."

With an absence of bombast, Truex roused the troops by establishing a realistic goal. Marine, he told stockholders, with $1.6 billion in deposits, was " 'Avis'—No. 2" to market leader Seattle-First National Bank, with $2.5 billion in deposits.

"I can't predict that we'll ever become No. 1" in size, "but there isn't any reason why it can't be our goal to become the No. 1 performer in terms of quality."

Reorganization

Before making these bold moves, Truex had to get the right people in the right places. By his own admission, he "lay in the weeds" for a few months, sizing up the bank, determining what it needed and whether that could be accomplished by the present structure of executives. Business psychologist Dr. Harry Coderre, a specialist in testing and evaluating personnel—whom Truex had known from B of A—was hired to do the same for NB of C employees. Several executives stood out in those tests, most notably Mangels, who had risen slowly and steadily through the ranks and was playing an ever-expanding role in the bank.

Coderre recalled he found a dedicated NB of C staff that had "tremendous loyalty to the bank." On the negative side, most staffers had not been encouraged to make decisions and lacked the entrepreneurial drive that

would be necessary in the coming era of banking deregulation. Compounded with that, many staff people felt they could not compete with Seattle-First, a situation that Truex called a "potentially fatal illness" in an interview in *American Banker*. Nevertheless, he added, "I think the talent is here, and I hope to see all key positions occupied by home-grown people, except in cases where need for a particular specialty forces us to go outside the bank."

A natural consensus builder, he told *American Banker* in a later interview: "It seemed best to avoid the flurry of unilateral actions that might very well have had the effect of turning off the senior officers who were already here. The last thing I wanted was to set up an attitude that would cause them to shrug and mutter to each other that I was going to do what I saw fit, no matter what, with the result that they might just as well keep their own counsel."

Mangels recalled that Truex "did all the things that a leader should do without destroying the many good things that this organization already possessed. He encouraged people to find a way to do things rather than being against change. He told us profit was important, growth was important, and that customer service was important."

Truex first tackled branch banking, which was the heart of the organization. The branches generally were managed by strong, local senior people who were accustomed to acting on their own, with little reporting responsibility, except directly to Carlson. Historically, the approval process at NB of C was laborious and Truex wanted to put more decision-making authority out in regions, a direction that had its seeds in the Faragher regime. The branches were weak at producing new business and selling new products and services. Truex asked key NB of C people to rate from one to 10 a suggested list of potential regional vice presidents—officers who could successfully oversee a group of 20 or 25 branches. Those people with the highest scores were later interviewed and tested by Coderre.

Borrowing a page from B of A's regional branch banking organization, NB of C set up the Washington Division, a six-region, statewide branch structure. Using improved accounting systems, each region was treated as a separate profit center with an annual goal and was staffed by qualified managers, loan administrators, personnel and operations supervisors, and business development officers. With every officer in every branch calling on customers and non-customers, there was an almost immediate increase in loans—monitored by quality control officers—as well as deposit volume and earnings.

The new system, coupled with the abolition of the Senior Loan Committee, speeded up the loan approval process. Truex felt that, in general, loan applications and problems should be resolved at the officer level. Because he believed the board of directors should be involved in policy matters rather than in loan decisions, Truex reduced the loan-review responsibilities of the board's executive committee and made the material going to the board less detailed and more meaningful.

The Washington Division was headed by Robert J. Svare, a senior vice president who had worked for the bank since 1947. Svare recounted: "It went into effect on October 1, 1974, and we didn't have a glitch because the people in this company were ready for something new—new authority, opportunities, trust. Everything—including the economic times—was right."

Asset and Liability Management

Good money management was high on the list of priorities. In an interview in *American Banker*, Truex said, "A bank must now know exactly the income and outgo, and be able to manage the spread a lot better than it did 10 or 20 years ago, or at any time in the history of the business when rates were more stable. Prices have to be watched and good judgments made about the price paid relative to terms committed. It's an inexact science, and one that we have to learn to handle a lot better."

The Asset and Liability Management Division, headed by Mangels, was formed in the fall of 1974, in order to develop asset allocation policy, manage money market functions, manage the portfolio, and determine and monitor loan policy and interest rates. Said a memorandum Truex and Faragher co-signed: "Our future profitability is tied closely to our ability to manage the spreads between the cost of acquisition and pricing of funds... Essentially, the mission of this new group is to make certain that funds used are acquired at minimum long-range cost and employed at maximum long-range yield."

Perhaps the biggest departure was borrowing from the Federal Reserve for the first time in the bank's history.

(Left) Asset and Liability Management head John D. Mangels.

(Right) Administrative head John F. Cockburn.

At the time, it was cheaper to borrow from the Fed than on the open market, but for many NB of C old-timers it was a traumatic shock because, under Carlson, the bank maintained its own financial well-being and never resorted to outside funds. Carlson used to say, very proudly, that he provided the liquidity off the assets side of the balance sheet. If the bank did not have sufficient deposit growth to take care of new loans, it would stop lending.

Under Truex the whole notion of liquidity changed. NB of C began to move from being a fixed-rate, long-term lender to being a floating-rate commercial bank. The bank began to look at the entire spectrum of the financial industry as a source of funding, and operated on the theory that the bank's ability to borrow was its liquidity. The result was that the bank and bancorporation began to borrow actively in short-term money markets.

John F. Cockburn, a longtime NB of C employee, was tapped to head the Administration Division, which combined several support functions, including operations and electronic data processing. Described in the 1974 annual report, this division's "improved computer capabilities are being developed based on the knowledge that automation not only provides better, faster service, but

also allows the bank to become more customer-oriented—to be more human."

Corporate Banking

Truex pledged not to bring any outsiders into the bank unless there was a demonstrable need that could not be filled from inside. Corporate banking was one of those areas in which specialists were needed. The bank had not been providing the services required to meet the specialized and complex financial needs of intermediate- and large-sized companies. Orville E. Melby, a Seattle native who had been a senior financial executive with several leading corporations, including Boeing, Continental Airlines and Martin-Marietta Corp., was brought in as senior vice president for corporate banking, which also included NB of C's Alaska Division and the Metropolitan, Correspondent and National groups. Melby had been on the other side of the desk as a bank customer, which helped bring a fresh, aggressive approach, as well as a sophisticated cash management system, to NB of C's corporate banking.

NB of C rapidly shed its parochial image. A staff of experienced bank employees was augmented by corporate finance specialists recruited from corporate banking giants Chase Manhattan, Bank of New York, First National Bank of Chicago and others. As Mangels described it: "One of the secrets to Truex is that he is able to blend very different backgrounds and personalities and do it very effectively."

The bank began to make greater inroads in the corporate community by increased lines of credit with companies such as General Motors, General Electric, Montgomery Ward and Weyerhaeuser. This was proof that a strong Pacific Northwest bank could deliver the kind of services required by international companies.

The Name Change

NB of C never had been strong in marketing, which was another area that needed immediate attention. "We should go out and get the business without being overly afraid of making mistakes," Truex told *American Banker*. In 1974, the bank hired a bank consulting firm, Newbury and Molinare of Winston-Salem, North Carolina, to prepare a report and present recommendations on how to improve Marine's structure.

Many of the problems were obvious. The holding company and the three major subsidiaries—NB of C, Coast Mortgage Company and Commerce Credit Company—lacked a common identifying name. The subsidiaries were "literally buzzing at one another," Truex told *The Seattle Times*, and "the bank tended to regard the holding company as some sort of foreign power." A name change would "get people thinking and remembering that we all have a common objective."

The idea of changing the name did not originate with Truex. From the time of the stock reorganization in 1969, the company felt the need to make the name of the parent company better known. "The National Bank of Commerce of Seattle" was too long and awkward to promote and advertise. Moreover, it was anything but unique; several other banks had similar names, including one in Tanzania. In January 1972, the directors had considered changing the name of the holding company to NB of C Bancorporation to end confusion in the Washington State customer and investor markets. The "NB of C" abbreviation was being used by consumers and younger bankers. But that decision, like many others, was put off until new management was in place.

When Truex came in, he knew "the name that needed to be changed was the bank, with the name of the holding company shaped to fit the bank. The bank was the promotion piece, the one that would be advertised and promoted, not the holding company."

Lippincott & Margulies set the parameters for the selection and market testing of a new name. Among the criteria: the name had to be short, memorable, related to the Pacific Northwest and not translatable to an obscenity in a foreign language. Some people wanted to maintain continuity by utilizing the name "Commerce." Personally, Truex told Lippincott & Margulies, he favored the name "Rainier," which had been suggested by a friend.

For some people, Rainier was too mundane. After all, they argued, there must have been 100 companies in the Seattle phone book beginning with Rainier, not the least of which was the Rainier Brewing Co., makers of Rainier Beer. After the announcement that Rainier would be the new name, the brewery asked the bank to reconsider, expressing concern about possible confusion in the sale of the brewery's over-the-counter securities in Seattle. Some local wags joked that NB of C would be known as the "no-deposit, no-return bank."

Lippincott & Margulies knew Rainier was going to be a tough sell to the board and to shareholders. The marketing company prepared a colorful presentation with banners and flashing lights and gave each director a crystal piece from Tiffany's etched with the name "Rainier Bank."

Robert F. Buck recalled: "Eventually, we were persuaded that Rainier was a symbol of solidity and beauty, which would distinguish Rainier from being just a Seattle bank. It was a geographic symbol that the entire state could relate to. For the rest of the nation, it would be a symbol of the Northwest. And for the Pacific Rim, it would be a symbol of Puget Sound and the State of Washington, the way that Mt. Fuji is a symbol of Japan."

The directors unanimously approved the name change on July 31, 1974, but that was just the beginning. The new corporate identity also required a two-thirds approval vote of stockholders, most of whom were local and had grown up with NB of C. It was not going to be an easy sell. Following the announcement of the proposed name "Rainier," Truex recalled: "The hate mail started to flow in." And Corporate Treasurer Ronald H. Mead remembered: "The name change was one of the most emotional things I've ever seen in the business community. It got

people upset. I would walk into a reception and I'd get five feet in the door and people would say, 'What are you people doing? How can you do this to my bank?'"

Truex, the outsider who had been in Seattle less than a year, said, "I would wake up in a cold sweat afraid this thing was going to go right down the drain, and I was going right down with it." Just in case the name change fell on its face, the bank got the assurance of the Comptroller of the Currency's office that it would not authorize the reuse of the name "The National Bank of Commerce of Seattle" for at least three years.

The company went on the offensive, taking a random poll and finding out that the mood in the community was more favorable than the mail indicated. In preparation for the crucial stockholders meeting in November, each stockholder was sent a magazine-sized brochure on heavy enamel stock explaining the reasons for the name change. The cover of the brochure was a dramatic, full-color photograph of Mt. Rainier at sunrise, which folded out to a panoramic 29 inches wide. Other materials included "The Most-asked Questions and Comments on the Name Change."

For the meeting itself, the bank recruited a number of important people to help the effort and diffuse any emotional arguments. Most prominent among them was Mrs. Ernest N. Patty, the widow of Andrew Price, Sr., the man who had named the bancorporation. Andrew Price, Jr., also favored the change. The stockholders overwhelmingly approved the name Rainier on November 7, 1974—one of the rare occasions when a bank underwent a name change without a merger or acquisition.

Officially, for stock reasons, the name of the holding company was changed first. On December 31, 1974, at the official close of business, NB of C formally changed its name to Rainier Bank. At 3:01 p.m., the 5-foot by 20-foot sign above the bank's head office at Second and Spring was lighted, becoming the first of some 169 of the bank's locations in the United States, Europe and East Asia to display the name. The subsidiaries were renamed Rainier Mortgage Company and Rainier Credit Company.

Advertising—other than a couple of announcements in *The Wall Street Journal*—was low key, initially. But in the first two quarters of 1975, the bank marketed the name through new services and products such as Rainier Bank bonds. Other institutional ads underscored the name "Rainier" by using familiar Seattle people, such as restaurateur Ivar Haglund and Michael Foster of the investment firm of Foster & Marshall.

RAINIER BANK

In 1974, Marine Bancorporation stockholders voted to change the name of the bank and holding company to Rainier National Bank and Rainier Bancorporation respectively. From left to right: Andrew Price, Jr., proposed the name change to the gathering of stockholders; Director W.J. Pennington seconded the name change; corporate Vice President and Treasurer Ronald H. Mead awaited the votes; and T. Robert Faragher, G. Robert Truex, Jr., and Andrew Price, Jr., announced the bank's new name.

The first physical signs of the change came with the removal of the old name from the bank's headquarters on Second Avenue.

Washington Trust Merger

The long-running battle over the merger with the Washington Trust Bank was finally resolved on June 26, 1974—coincidentally, the same day that Truex was named president and chief executive officer of the holding company and the bank, and Faragher was named chairman. The U.S. Supreme Court voted five to three in favor of the merger, ruling against the Department of Justice's antitrust theory that a merger should be barred if it might reduce future competition even though it did not appear likely to affect competition at present. The majority based its ruling primarily on the fact that Washington State banking laws sharply restricted the ability of NB of C to open or acquire branches in Spokane. That ruling weakened the Justice Department's contention that NB of C would still compete in Spokane even if the Washington Trust merger were blocked.

Prior to the final Supreme Court decision, Truex asked Corporate Treasurer Mead to analyze the acquisition. Mead had worked on the details of the merger from the accounting side when he worked for the accounting firm of Haskins & Sells before joining Marine. After several months of examining the economics of the deal, particularly the dilution to Marine's shareholder base, Mead took the position that the premium was about twice what it should be. Mead recalled: "The pricing would significantly dilute our shareholder base, taking away from us the earnings-per-share growth we wanted to have going forward." A further study by the San Francisco office of the

Through logo and symbols, the bank moved quickly to establish its strong Pacific Northwest identity and its relationship with Mt. Rainier.

investment banking firm of Blyth Eastman Dillon & Co. corroborated Mead's findings. Both reports and recommendations were taken to the board along with the finding that the price was too high. At the same meeting in which the name change was voted on, the board made the decision not to go forward with the merger.

Maxwell Carlson Resigns

On September 16, 1974, Carlson resigned as a director of both NB of C and Marine, and as honorary chairman of Marine. Price retired as chairman of the board of the bancorporation, and was succeeded by Faragher. Truex was president and chief executive of both the holding company and the bank; Faragher was chairman of both.

Over the previous few months, Carlson had been quietly removing his personal effects and papers from the bank. On his last day, with a characteristic absence of fanfare, he handed his keys to his secretary, Winifred Stedman, and abruptly left the building, the company and his business life. (Despite his childhood years of ill health, he lived to be 81, passing away in September 1987.)

Carlson's resignation letter took on an unintentionally ironic tone, warning directors not to permit one individual to dominate its operations. He also stressed that "it is imperative that the quality of the bank's assets be preserved even at the expense of current earnings if necessary and that the bank's liquidity not be jeopardized by overly ambitious asset and liability management." Nevertheless, he added "the Carlson family continued…

to augment its investment in the common stock of Marine Bancorporation."

It was a good investment because 1974, in spite of all its changes, was a record year for Rainier. Consolidated net operating earnings increased 19 percent to an all-time high of $13.8 million. And for the first time in history, deposits exceeded $2 billion. Net loan losses were virtually nil.

In the International Division, the bank opened a new full-service office in the Marinouchi district of Tokyo, the first branch established by a Pacific Northwest bank in that city. International also regionalized its operations by creating Asia-Pacific, Americas and Europe-Middle East-Africa groups.

Increased efforts to recruit and develop the talents of women and minorities resulted in a 59-percent growth in the bank's female officer staff since 1973. During the same period, there was a 91-percent increase in the number of minority officers. More than 10 percent of the bank's total staff then comprised minorities, as compared to a state minority population of only 7 percent.

As good as those figures were, the past proved to be no more than prologue because the new team at the bank with the new name had only just begun to make its impact.

Maxwell Carlson.

G. Robert Truex, Jr.,
christened the last steel beam
in 1974 before it was lifted
into place atop the 40-story
Rainier Bank Tower.

G. Robert Truex, Jr., virtually remade Rainier Bank. He forged a new style that mirrored that of aggressive money center banks. While setting lofty, but closely monitored, production goals, he never lost sight of his principal objective—increased profitability. He stressed more precise asset and liability management, and he instituted tighter internal accounting procedures that exposed millions of dollars in under-invested funds. Deposited funds were more quickly converted to earning assets and as a result, within a few years, the bank more than doubled its net interest income.

The new Rainier Bank began to purchase liquidity and to fund itself in any market in which it could raise money, nationally and internationally. For the first time, Rainier sold certificates of deposit in the national market.

Real estate lending activities of both Rainier Bank and the mortgage company were brought together, giving borrowers innovative and more diverse financing programs. Soon, both the mortgage and credit companies were contributing significantly to the consolidated net income.

At the same time, the loan portfolio took on a more profitable mix. Long-term, fixed-rate real estate loan totals were allowed to decline, and the funds were redirected into higher returning instalment and corporate loans; the latter total jumped 100 percent.

Rainier refined its wholesale

banking efforts and created the World Banking Division, which was a merger of corporate, correspondent and international banking. Rainier expanded its Boeing business significantly and picked up business from Pan American World Airways, Aloha Airlines of Hawaii, Western Airlines, Alaska Airlines, Campbell Soup, Georgia Pacific, Green Giant, Weyerhaeuser and International Telephone and Telegraph. International customers included Kawasaki and Nippon Steel of Japan.

One special account was the Seattle Seahawks which, in 1974, was a newborn expansion National Football League franchise. Executive Vice President Robert F. Buck and then-Vice President Gordon F. Givens secured the account, which Givens characterized as a "very visible project—an example of what Truex wanted us to do."

At the same time, the bank began to pursue aggressively the business of Northwest "middle-market" companies—firms with annual sales between $5 million and $250 million—although most of the market topped out at $25 million. A Rainier-commissioned study of the middle market—compiled by Allan F. Munro of the Connecticut firm Greenwich Research—found more than 700 companies in Washington State with sales of $5 million or more, and 300 with sales over $12 million. Orville E. Melby recalled that the report "showed how poorly the market thought of Rainier Bank. Seattle-First

World Banking head Orville E. Melby.

Head coach Jack Patera confers with quarterback Jim Zorn during the first game of the Seahawks 1976 inaugural season.

In both retail and wholesale banking, Rainier unveiled new programs. The advertising budget increased, as did the creativity. The bank won national awards with an ad campaign that included a signature of social consciousness: "So start your savings campaign today with Rainier—or any other bank for that matter."

owned the market. So, we geared our whole corporate effort to satisfy the weaknesses we saw in the report." Rainier courted that market with new services and programs, as well as seminars on subjects like taxes and foreign exchange, which were open to both customers and noncustomers.

Rainier added a new profit center in 1975 when it formed Rainier Bank Leasing, Inc., a wholly owned subsidiary, which brought together the leasing activities of the subsidiaries. David I. Williams, vice president and manager, was recruited from Wells Fargo, and spearheaded new business through leasing a wide variety of equipment to an equally wide variety of businesses—from potato packing sheds to brain scanners to blast hole drills. He was a typical example of the young, aggressive specialists recruited from outside the old NB of C organization.

Public Debt

In order to strengthen the capital bases of the subsidiaries and to add some capital in the bank, Rainier initiated its first-ever public issue of debt securities in 1975. Under Truex, Rainier took a building-block approach to the capital allocation of the subsidiaries, so that their liability and capital structures met or exceeded industry-wide standards. The ideal was to maintain balance and growth of all subsidiaries relative to the company's total resources.

Historically, the activities and expansion of the mortgage and credit companies had been funded by commercial paper but, as Mead recalled, "we couldn't keep expanding these companies with 30- and 40-day commercial paper. If anything happened in the financial markets you had to have liquidity; you had to have some longer-term funds."

Management debated whether to go with public financing or private placement; the latter had been done in 1973 with the Traveler's Insurance Co. But a compelling argument was that a successful bond offering also brought with it a higher national profile for Rainier Bancorporation.

After earning "A" ratings from Standard & Poor's and Moody's, a Rainier team headed by Truex, Mangels and Mead spread the corporation's story through a series of meetings with analysts throughout the Pacific Northwest and in New York. In July 1975, the bank marketed $30 million in 10-year, 9.5-percent notes, which qualified for listing on the New York Stock Exchange.

Mead recalled: "The 9.5-percent rate we had to pay the national market was a hefty rate. I was sensitive to that extra half we had to pay. As it turned out, it was one of the best moves we ever made because later on, the rates went way up. It gave us a debt-capital base for further growth."

Out of that $30 million note issue, $10 million was loaned to the bank on a subordinated term basis, and $8.5 million was advanced to the mortgage company and $11 million to the credit company, also on a term basis.

An Upward Curve

In the 1973 annual report, Truex said it would take about three years to become as profitable as the nation's more successful one-bank holding companies. But he surpassed that target. Thanks to the bank's bold strokes, net operating earnings advanced 35 percent, reaching $18.6 million, and 1975 became the most profitable year ever. Effective asset and liability management, Truex believed, was the most important factor in Rainier's 26-percent increase in net interest income, a gain of $21 million—$12 million from improved margins, and $9 million from increased volume of earning assets.

In the first three years of the Truex regime, equity grew by $35 million to $146 million, a 31-percent jump. Return on average assets increased by nearly half to 0.72 percent, and return on average equity jumped by more than half, to 13.7 percent. Net loan losses were the lowest of the nation's top 50 banks in 1975—0.096 percent. By the middle of 1976, Rainier moved from 86th to 39th in earnings, 50th in assets. The monthly over-the-counter trading volume of Rainier stock doubled.

"Black Monday"

Management was keenly aware that the bank was overstaffed but, for a couple of years, while the bank's computer capacity and data processing facilities were expanded, personnel decisions were postponed, in the hope that natural attrition would solve the problem. However, high operating costs continued to be a drag on Rainier's profits.

Unfortunately, attrition was not occurring in the right places, and Rainier was compelled to lay off 252 workers. The one-time staff reduction took place on Monday, January 15, 1976, and resulted in an unexpected public relations flap. All employees were supposed to have

The 1976 board of directors: (Standing, from left) Joseph E. Muckley, John D. Mangels, T. Robert Faragher, Donald E. Schaake, John C. Mundt, Arne T. Lervick, Winston D. Brown, Louis Arrigoni, Francis G. Crane, James A. Walsh, George F. Vance, G. Robert Truex, Jr., and Bryant R. Dunn. (Seated, from left) Stanley D. Golub, W.J. Pennington, Marjorie W. Evans and L.P. Himmelman. Absent: C.M. Ambrose, Jr., Wallace R. Bunn, Wylie M. Hemphill, Henry C. Isaacson, Jr., C. Calvert Knudsen, John R. Meyer and Andrew Price, Jr.

Consulting with G. Robert Truex, Jr., in establishing Rainier Bank's social policy statement was Bank Director Marjorie W. Evans, who had served Truex in a similar role during his tenure at the Bank of America.

senior officers. It was modeled after the Truex-designed program at B of A. The new department was responsible for developing standards, formulating ongoing programs, monitoring performance and ensuring that good public policy would be an integral part of the company's business.

In 1977, Rainier adopted a five-point social policy statement built around the importance of community affairs, consumerism, education, affirmative action and contributions. The statement defined the social framework in which the corporation and its subsidiaries would do business. The preamble read:

> *To achieve the goal of providing the greatest value for our shareholders, Rainier Bancorporation must fulfill its obligation to be a leading citizen of the community. Our commitment to the public interest is directed to the long-term benefit of both the community and the company. All company activities will meet these standards.*

The social policy program included financial assistance for remodeling older homes through a neighborhood Home Loan Center on Seattle's Capitol Hill. The bank also developed an affirmative lending program geared to assist small minority-owned businesses with special credit needs.

By the end of 1977, women and minorities represented 41 percent of bank management. Minorities comprised 12 percent of employees, compared to 8.2 percent for the entire state.

been terminated personally by their supervisors, but communications broke down, and some workers learned of the news upon returning from lunch when they found letters of dismissal on their desks. The episode generated negative newspaper headlines—a rarity in the public relations-minded Truex era.

Truex later supported the action in *California Business*: "What we didn't want to happen was for the layoffs to come in bits and drabs and create the feeling of an ax hanging over the place."

This problem was short-lived. Morale and margins improved, and Rainier soon had the highest-paid tellers in the state.

That same year, the bank established a social policy department and a supporting social policy committee of

Rainier Bank Tower architect

Minoru Yamasaki.

1977: *Towering Changes*

The year 1977 was one of the most significant in the bank's history.

A new 215,000-square-foot, two-story operations center south of Seattle marked a major step toward consolidation of administrative and support offices. It brought together 30 departments that had been scattered about in 20 locations, including information services, storage and branch supplies, administrative offices, systems development, operations, purchasing and bank card services. The center also served as the servicing base for the mortgage company accounts.

The operations center housed an internally developed computer model and a new wave of data processing specialists, who were recruited to handle greater, more sophisticated business, particularly in short-term and long-term liquidity planning. These moves represented the action behind a recurring Truex message: "The bank that isn't up to date on data processing is the one that's going to fall by the wayside."

Perhaps the biggest news of 1977—literally and figuratively—was the move into the 40-story Rainier Bank Tower, which was the dominant structure of the Rainier Square complex in downtown Seattle.

This giant step culminated a process that began in 1970 when the head office building committee, originally chaired by Faragher and later Buck—working with Director Wylie M. Hemphill—hired architect Minoru Yamasaki of Troy, Michigan. Locally, Yamasaki had been the archi-

tect for the IBM Building and Seattle's Pacific Science Center. Nationally, his projects included the Century Plaza Hotel in Los Angeles and the 110-story twin towers of the World Trade Center in New York. The committee and Carlson, who wanted as many local people involved as possible, were impressed not only with Yamasaki's credentials, but also with the fact that he was of Japanese descent, born and raised in Seattle, and had attended the University of Washington.

Faragher told the press, "The influence of Far Eastern architecture on Mr. Yamasaki's design is important to the bank and to Seattle as the city becomes more and more the gateway to the Orient. The bank's growth and development in markets around the Pacific Rim… blend beautifully with Mr. Yamasaki's design concept."

At the time, the company had to choose between two sites for the new building—either its aging headquarters at Second and Spring, where it owned the entire block, or a

block it had recently acquired between Sixth and Seventh avenues and University and Union streets. (The latter would later be the site of the One and Two Union Square buildings.) The bank was contacted by the property management company, University Properties (Unico), which suggested a third alternative—the block between Fourth and Fifth avenues and University and Union— which was kitty-corner from Yamasaki's IBM Building, and which became its ultimate location.

Yamasaki wanted the design of the bank building to relate to the curve of the arches in the IBM Building. At a lunch meeting with Buck and other committee members, Yamasaki drew an outline of a tower, which stood on a pedestal with reverse curves.

"These curves correspond to the curves of the IBM Building," Yamasaki explained. "As an architect, that's a pleasing correlation." The pedestal design featured a structure that cantilevered out from an elevator shaft and

In preparation for the bank tower's construction, the venerable White-Henry-Stuart Building was razed.

The Rainier Bank Tower was opened in October 1977 and was celebrated with the hanging of a controversial "sky sculpture" from the top of its pedestal.

equipment space that would rise 12 stories above the ground; the finished product measured 56 by 74 feet at the ground and curved out to 121 by 140 feet at the base. The design would reduce the foundation cost because the support for the tower came from the center of the building rather than the outside corners.

At the same time, the design would allow light and air to reach the ground level. Yamasaki believed these features would be appreciated by Seattle activists, who were fighting an emotional, well-publicized campaign for saving the White-Henry-Stuart Building, a venerable structure that would be razed in order to build the Tower.

The corporation took formal occupancy at 9:37 a.m. on Monday, October 10, 1977. Truex cut the ribbon with a sword once owned by the legendary British Navy Admiral Peter Rainier, and the bank opened its new Main Office in Rainier Square, its 122nd branch in the state. With the opening, Rainier consolidated under one roof nearly 100 corporate and bank operations, representing about 600 employees.

The marketing benefits were almost immediate. Soon after the opening of the building, Rainier raised its profile by hosting a luncheon for the Seattle investment community and a group of out-of-town bank analysts who were on the West Coast to attend a major B of A presentation in San Francisco.

The following year's annual meeting in March drew a record attendance of shareholders, attracted by promised tours of the Tower.

And the building's aesthetics won the approval of a skeptical city. Its clean lines, open-space airiness and landscaped promenades, shops and restaurants made the Tower and the entire Rainier Square project a valued and people-oriented addition to the community.

The Rainier Bank Tower sits atop a 12-story steel and concrete pedestal.

Wall Street's "Battle of Seattle"

In the first five years of the Truex regime, earnings grew at a compounded rate of 21 percent a year. On a per-share basis, that was the best record of the nation's 50 largest bank holding companies. The stock rose more than 200 percent to about $25 a share (on a pre-1984-split basis)—the best performance of any large U.S. bank. Rainier's loan portfolio contained strong assets developed from the Corporate Banking Group. These results were helped by a robust Northwest economy fueled by construction, fishing, agriculture and trade through Puget Sound ports, as well as the boom following the completion of the trans-Alaska pipeline in 1978.

As regional business activity continued to expand, Washington State experienced record levels of employment and personal income and attracted almost 100,000 new residents a year. From 1973 to 1977, the population of Washington grew at twice the national average rate and, in 1977 alone, 90,000 jobs were added to the state's rolls. Personal income far surpassed the national average.

The flip side of Rainier's strong performance was a reduction in the bank's equity-to-asset ratio. In spring 1978, management, with the approval of the board, opted to raise equity. When Rainier's New York investment bankers flew to Seattle to work on the equity offering, they noticed that they were sharing the flight with another group of investment bankers from a rival New York firm. The question on the minds of both camps: "What are all these New York investment bankers doing in Seattle?"

Rainier's prospectus was quickly written, approved by the board and filed with the Securities and Exchange Commission in Washington, D.C. The day after the filing, Rainier management found out what those other investment bankers were doing on that flight: Seattle-First (Seafirst) announced it would be filing its own equity offering the next day.

Most observers predicted that Seafirst's issue of 1.3 million shares would muscle out Rainier's 1-million-share offering. But that was not the case. Both issues were snapped up so quickly by investors that Rainier and Seafirst each increased their initial offering by 200,000 shares. The successful twin offerings briefly turned the attention of the investment community to Seattle. During that time, Truex was flying around the country to meetings of analysts, speaking with his singular aplomb about the Rainier story.

Rainier gained almost $29 million in additional equity, which it used to fund expansion of its loan portfolio by 26 percent in 1978 and another 19 percent in 1979.

But beyond the bottom line, the showdown with Seafirst—"The Battle of Seattle," as it was dubbed by *American Banker*—marked the bank's coming of age in the eyes of bank stock analysts and institutional investors. Despite the fact that Rainier's assets were $3.5 billion, compared with Seafirst's $5.9 billion, "in the minds of investors," one analyst was quoted in *Business Week*, "there is now little difference between the two companies."

As Mead recalled, this feeling "filtered to the marketplace, to the customers and to our account officers. It created a total momentum for the whole organization."

Organization and Reorganization

Truex was keenly aware that companies are living organisms composed of interdependent parts in a perpetual state of subtle and not-so-subtle evolution. "We've organized and reorganized," he told business writer Elliot Marple. "Organization changes all the time. Some people here have trouble with that. They don't understand that an organization is a thing that suits your needs at the moment, the needs of the marketplace and the talents of the people. Every time you print an organization directory it is obsolete as soon as it comes off the press."

In 1977, when Faragher retired, Truex became chairman and chief executive officer of the bank, while remaining president and CEO of the bancorporation. Truex said, "If Bob Faragher had not been there [as chairman following Carlson] I would have had to invent him. He laid most of the groundwork before I arrived and made my job a whole lot easier."

Mangels, who had become vice chairman of the corporation in 1975, succeeded Truex as president of the bank, while continuing as vice chairman of the corporation. In April 1978, branch and consumer-oriented activities were realigned under C.W. Strong, Jr., who was elected president of Rainier Bancorporation and vice chairman of the bank. In 1980, when the bank realigned the wholesale, commercial and retail banking operations, Melby was named vice chairman of the bank.

T. Robert Faragher.

Truex was not making change for change's sake. As he tinkered with the Rainier machine, he found he could live with a certain amount of organizational disorganization by allowing capable people to do their jobs in their own way. Such "controlled freedom" was one of the qualities that attracted bright young bankers with entrepreneurial spirit to Rainier.

Michael J. Coie, Rainier's executive vice president, recalled, "Bob had an amazing knack to sense when to step on the accelerator and when to change the direction of the company."

Truex frequently set people in competition with one another to come up with innovative answers to perplexing problems.

In Melby, the self-acknowledged non-banker, and

C. R. Chadwick.

Mangels, the quintessential banker and credit man, Truex found two men who were perfect counterbalances, resulting in a highly creative dynamic tension within the organizational hierarchy.

Stanley D. Savage, a vice chairman, marveled at Melby's "ability to deal with and relate to the customer. He was able to execute the strategy that Truex brought to corporate banking." As Vice Chairman David I. Williams saw it: "Melby helped us move faster to where we needed to go. He could roll the dice—partly because of his sales background, partly because he had Bob Truex's ear."

Mangels, a strong, principled banker, had Truex's other ear. As a man who began his career at NB of C as a part-time teller and 30 years later became vice chairman, his depth of experience gave him a unique perspective on the organization. Truex affectionately nicknamed him "Oracle"—which *Webster's Dictionary* defines as "an infallible authority." Truex described Mangels as "one of the brightest people I've ever known. He throws a word on the table and waits to see if it will grow."

C. R. Chadwick, a retired vice chairman, noted, "John has the ability to listen to you and decide whether you are right or wrong. If you know what you're doing, you can go for it; if you don't, you're in trouble."

For Truex, who managed by consensus, this competition of ideas and philosophies generated from different backgrounds brought out the best in both men—and the best in the bank.

Entering the 1980s, the mettle of these men and all Rainier executives would be acutely tested. The events of

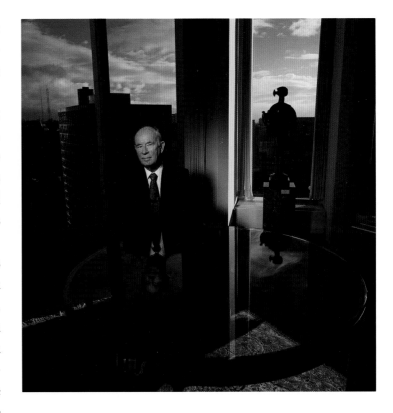

the next decade were destined to have profound and lasting effects on Rainier Bank and the landscape of American banking.

Nationally, Rainier had become a known quantity. *Business Week* called Rainier one of "20 stocks to watch in the financial revolution" in a 1980 article on interstate banking investment opportunities. Its financial performance during the last five years of the 1970s ranked in the top three among the nation's biggest regional banks and holding companies.

The Rainier Bank Tower's 12-story pedestal at Fifth and University in the evening.

CHAPTER FIVE

When Banking Changed Forever

(From left) G. Robert Truex, Jr., John D. Mangels, C.W. Strong, Jr., and Orville E. Melby.

For bankers, the '80s became the Decade of Deregulation, the era when the nature of banking products and services was forever altered, and the distinctions between financial institutions and traditional competition were permanently blurred.

Unshackled from existing laws and regulations, non-bank competitors, such as national retailers, brokers and insurance companies—built up through strategic mergers and acquisitions—crashed the bankers' game and redefined it. The most notable of these new heavily muscled players were American Express, which merged with Shearson Loeb Rhoades; Sears, which bought Dean Witter Reynolds and Coldwell Banker; and Prudential Insurance, which acquired Bache Securities.

These financial giants were armed with established, sophisticated computer and communication networks, manned by trained, commissioned sales veterans, and posted in existing retail outlets. Without the tether of banking regulations and regulators, they could do what banks were barred from doing: provide financial products and services regardless of interstate boundaries at rates dictated by the market. Consumers could choose from money market funds, savings banks' NOW (negotiable orders of withdrawal) accounts and credit unions' shared drafts (all of which helped undermine the old banking maxim: Checking accounts do not bear interest).

Merrill Lynch's biggest salvo was its Cash Management Account (CMA), which combined features of traditional brokerage accounts and bank accounts. Although not insured by the federal government, CMAs, which

American Banker called "the era's foremost product innovation," paid higher interest than savings accounts.

The new financial conglomerates could outprice the banks, which were squeezed between rising inflation and shrinking net interest revenue, traditionally the key component of bank earnings. Banks began redirecting their activities toward greater dependence on non-interest income, such as fees and commissions on transactions, and what had once been deemed non-banking businesses, such as financial planning.

Bankers argued that they were competing on an unlevel financial playing field, and pleaded the case for the opportunity to deliver competitive products and services, and across state lines—i.e., through interstate banking.

The Carter administration began to address the obsolescence of federal banking law with a flurry of legislation, the most notable of which was the Depository Institutions Deregulation and Monetary Control Act of 1980. This bill, which took effect at the start of 1981, reshaped the financial services industry by phasing out interest rate controls on deposits; lifting ceilings on mortgage loan interest rates; and legalizing interest-bearing NOW checking accounts for banks. The act also imposed reserve requirements on all depository institutions, not just banks that were members of the Federal Reserve.

Some larger banks turned the tables by invading their rivals' own turf. B of A purchased Charles Schwab & Co., the discount brokerage service. Security Pacific formed a brief association with Fidelity Brokerage Services before purchasing Kahn & Co. of Memphis, Tennessee. By 1983, according to a *Business Week* article, about 600 banks and thrifts had joined forces with established discounters.

Furthermore, sympathetic legislators were introducing bills in Congress that would allow banks to set up and advise mutual funds and underwrite municipal revenue bonds. (Banks were already allowed to underwrite general obligation bonds.) Congress, however, steadfastly disallowed banks to underwrite corporate securities.

Non-bank loans increased at the same time. Large corporations, which had their own strong credit ratings, were less likely to borrow from banks when they could use other tools, such as commercial paper. Investment banks, which matched providers and users of capital, began taking away business from commercial banks, which were in turn spurred to establish investment banking divisions.

Interstate Banking

Interstate banking came closer to reality when a 1981 amendment to the federal Bank Holding Company Act allowed individual states to decide whether to permit out-of-state bank corporations to establish footholds within the states' borders.

In 1981, while the Alaska state legislature worked on an amendment that would allow an out-of-state bank holding company to acquire a failing Alaska bank, Rainier tried to take over Security National Bank of Anchorage but was rebuffed when Alaska's lawmakers tabled the legislation. In 1982, however, Alaska enacted the most liberal bank-entry regulations in the United States, and

Rainier acquired the outstanding stock of Peoples Bank & Trust of Anchorage, a small bank with assets of $51 million.

At the same time, Rainier Bank opened an international banking facility (which accepted deposits and extended credit to foreign residents) in Seattle and an Edge Act international banking office in Portland, Oregon.

Following interstate banking revisions in the state of Alaska in 1982, Rainier purchased Peoples Bank & Trust of Anchorage.

During this period, Rainier Bank made the acquisition of the $20 million commercial loan portfolio of Valley National Bank in Salinas, California; the leasing company opened offices in Los Angeles and Houston; and the mortgage company bought existing offices in Phoenix and Sierra Vista, Arizona.

Locally, Seattle's growth as a regional financial center brought about new competition from large out-of-state bank holding companies, including Security Pacific, B of A and Citicorp, all of which set up offices in Seattle in the early 1980s.

Rainier Bank management suffered from no delusions about the future of banking, and made it known in an annual report message: "Banks can no longer assume profitability, or even survival, by merely offering the traditional products and services of the past." Rainier people aggressively went after business, motivated by sales and service.

Rainier was already following a strategy suggested in a 1983 *Business Week* article: "Deregulation will challenge virtually all U.S. banks with the enormous tasks of overhauling their organizational structure, picking their market niches, and turning managers into marketers and strategic planners… and entrepreneurs who can hack it in a deregulated environment."

Regionally, Rainier finally established itself in three important Washington State markets: Spokane, with a swap of five Rainier branches for five Old National Bank branches; Snohomish County, with its merger with the 10-branch Bank of Everett; and Tacoma, with the acquisition of a branch of the North Pacific Bank.

Economic Slowdown

The Washington State economy took a pounding on almost every front in the early 1980s. Boeing slowed down production, the forest products industry was in a recession, and agriculture and fishing were fraught with problems. The associated drop in sales tax revenue forced the state to cut spending and employment. Jobs fell by 60,000 between May 1981 and May 1982 and, after a decade of rapid population growth, people were moving out of Washington. Furthermore, the national perception of investing in Washington was hurt by the unfavorable publicity surrounding the failing bond investments in the Washington Public Power Supply System nuclear power plant construction.

Faced with double-digit inflation in excess of 20 percent, Washington State bankers heatedly argued against the state's usury law, which limited consumer loans, including credit cards and residential mortgages, to a 12-percent rate. Bankers claimed interest ceilings curtailed funding for the residential housing market, which hurt the state's important lumber and home construction industries. In 1981, bankers got some relief with a new law that fixed the interest-rate ceiling on consumer loans and bank cards at 4 percentage points above the six-month Treasury bill coupon-equivalent rate. Branches began offering direct loans between 18 and 19.02 percent.

Rainier's consolidated net operating earnings in 1980

increased only 3 percent to $39,386,000, compared with $38,385,000 a year earlier. On the positive side, the slowdown in domestic earnings growth was largely offset by excellent performance in the bank's international offices, thanks to increased earning assets and improved net interest spread. In 1981, consolidated net operating earnings increased 12 percent to $44,096,000.

A Bank Called Penn Square

With the Northwest's basic industries in the doldrums, Rainier's National Banking Group began to build up its domestic loan portfolio outside the region by pursuing the business of *Fortune* 1,000 companies. At the time, with soaring inflation, many bankers were lending feverishly to the energy and real estate industries. Aggressive lenders placed their bets on inflation, enticed by appealing fees and spreads—though they sometimes overlooked traditional banking practices by lending without gathering all the facts and making judgments based more on potential return than security.

In 1981, oil prices were nearing their peak and megamillion-dollar drilling rigs were being built at an unprecedented rate. Around that time, Seattle-First National Bank (Seafirst) began lending money for exploration and oil drilling equipment in Texas and Oklahoma. The Pacific Northwest's largest bank grew larger, as energy loans swelled its asset ledger. Banking giants such as Continental Illinois Bank and Trust and Chase Manhattan Bank were doing the same, on an even grander scale.

The bank began to focus on energy lending. Retired Executive Vice President John F. Cockburn recalled, "With all of the other sizable banks doing it, and with Alaska being an increasingly large player, we all decided it was the thing to do, but with expertise and caution."

In the early spring of that year, Jeffrey Anderson, an energy-lending expert, was hired from Security Pacific's Energy Loan Group to start an energy-lending program for the bank.

To provide the needed technical expertise, Rainier hired a perceptive young woman named Sally Jewell, just three years after she had received her B.A. in mechanical engineering from the University of Washington. Jewell had learned the basics of the petroleum business as an oil field engineer for Mobil Oil in southern Oklahoma. She moved from there to engineering planning in Mobil's Denver office, where she worked out expense budgets and production projections for Mobil fields in 42 states. Later, she evaluated acquisitions for the oil giant.

Rainier's new Energy-lending Group planned a two-pronged attack, Jewell recalled: "One, to look for big banks, such as Republic Bank [now First Republic Corp.] or Union Bank, which were putting together deals because they were in areas that needed capital. We could take a big enough piece to be worthwhile for them. Two, to look for small banks in capital-poor areas." These banks had borrowers who exceeded their lending capacity and needed other banks to participate with new financing.

Penn Square National Bank, a young bank headquartered in an Oklahoma City shopping mall, was an example

Rainier Bank did invest in the "oil patch," but it was cautious. The bank made petro-loans in Alaska, including financing for this drilling rig for Westward Well Service Company, a joint venture of two Alaska native corporations, NANA Regional Corporation and Bristol Bay Native Corporation.

of the latter. Penn Square had a lending limit of only $1 million but it was able to sell hundreds of millions of dollars in energy loans to a "Who's Who in Banking" roster of participating banks, including Seafirst, whose portfolio was fattened with energy loans and whose bottom line showed enviable earnings figures.

Early in 1982, Anderson and Jewell flew to Oklahoma City to check out, firsthand, the Penn Square operation. Jewell recalled: "The first time I met them, they brought us $30 million worth of deals. We told them to wait a minute! Jeff and I took a logical, methodical approach, which is the way Rainier does things. I went through the engineering information, Jeff went through the credit files, and we both toured their documentation area and collateral control. We found their packages weren't complete. On the surface, they looked like a good piece of business, but not after you asked basic questions."

Meanwhile, Rainier Bank management and direc-

tors were wondering aloud whether the bank should emulate Seafirst. Vice Chairman David I. Williams recounted: "Once, Bob Truex asked me: 'Are we doing what we should be doing?' I said, 'I think so.' " Yet, Williams couldn't help but question his own judgment. "People were making money hand over fist. If the price of oil kept going up, we were stupid. And yet, you just had to look at each deal, and ask yourself: Do I understand it?"

At the end of June 1982, Jewell gave presentations to Rainier senior management and the board of directors, listing tens of millions of dollars in potential energy loans from Penn Square and other sources and the rationale for turning down those loans. She also listed the deals in which Seafirst was involved and why those deals, in her opinion, made no sense. "My timing was impeccable," Jewell remarked. "My presentation was on June 29, and Penn Square failed on July 5."

When the dust had settled, the failure of Penn Square

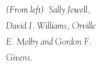

(From left) Sally Jewell, David I. Williams, Orville E. Melby and Gordon F. Givens.

nearly toppled Continental, which was saved by a $4.5 billion bailout by the Federal Deposit Insurance Corporation—at that time the largest rescue in banking history.

Seafirst lost $91 million in 1982. They announced loan losses for 1983 would be around $150 million. (Jewell had run the potential Seafirst losses through her desktop computer and had come up with the staggering total exposure of $400 million, which provoked disbelieving chuckles around the Rainier energy loan department.) Jewell was uncannily accurate. Seafirst took a loss of $456 million in 1983 and was dangling on the precipice.

The Northwest's largest bank was saved from ruin by a hastily passed Washington State law that allowed out-of-state banks to buy failing Washington banks. B of A was Seafirst's white knight, buying the company for $400 million. As Philip L. Zweig wrote in his book *Belly Up*, a

Rainier Bank has $400,000,000 to lend.

Imagine the possibilities. There's never been a better time to get a loan from Rainier Bank. So see a Rainier personal banker today. With $400,000,000 to lend, nothing's impossible. RAINIERBANK *We're Involved*

chronicle of the Penn Square fiasco: "What could have been the biggest bank failure in American history became the largest interstate takeover."

Rainier, which spread out its $20 million energy loan portfolio over 10 firms, was saved from a similar fate because, in Williams' words, "everyone did his or her job, and the system worked. There was a process and you have to work your way through that process."

Orville E. Melby, Rainier's world banking head, commented, "Maybe you could say we were lucky, but I don't think so. We had some good checks and balances in the organization. We were aggressive, but we were solid."

Jewell gave much of the credit to Givens. "Gordon is fantastic at zeroing in on the important things. He's got incredible insights."

Givens, for his part, claimed, "I don't think I ever turned down a deal. They were turned down by Sally Jewell, David Williams and Jeff Anderson. Under our culture, we have a drive to understand, to get all the facts, and look the guy in the eye and be able to feel comfortable that he knows what he's doing and he's going to pay you back. That's why the loans were turned down long before they got to me—and that's the way it should be."

This fortuitous advertisement coincided with Seafirst's announced $456 million loss.

After the Fall

Rainier Bank corporate counsel Bruce A. Koppe.

Seafirst's failure was not in Rainier's best interests. In fact, Rainier offered a sizable loan to keep Seafirst liquid. The offer was refused.

Rainier also carefully evaluated the acquisition of Seafirst in 1982. John D. Mangels recalled: "We had a series of long meetings to consider it, but we were only guessing at how deep their problems were. Even if it was as good as we hoped, it would have required betting the whole bundle on the transaction. We would have had to borrow so much money to make the acquisition that it would have kept this company from being a stable organization."

Rainier fiercely fought the Washington State bank bill, which applied only to failing banks. It had been hastily written and passed to allow B of A to purchase Seafirst and it also began the process of interstate banking in Washington. Rainier's opposition, however, had nothing to do with interstate banking in general or B of A in particular. In fact, the contrary was true. Bruce Koppe, Rainier's corporate counsel, recounted: "We wanted an open interstate banking law. We wanted it open all the way. We told the legislature we wanted the same rights to be acquired as Seafirst. We didn't see why failure should be rewarded."

Two years later, in May 1985, the state legislature approved an amendment to the banking law, which authorized interstate banking to take effect July 1, 1987. Lawmakers felt the two-year period would allow for an

"organized transition" into this brave new banking world.

In the wake of Seafirst's predicament, Rainier, of course, took optimum advantage—just at a time when Rainier needed it. G. Robert Truex, Jr., told *The Seattle*

Times: "When disaster befell them, their reputation was diminished and ours was enhanced... We decided to go after the jugular—to get every bit of business we could from them."

Coinciding with a rebound in most of the key elements of the Northwest economy, Rainier made $100 million worth of commitments in 1983 to former Seafirst customers, and dramatically cut the gap in commercial loans. National money markets called Rainier with offers that in the past probably would have gone to Seafirst.

By the end of 1984, Rainier had assets of $7.8 billion compared to Seafirst's $9 billion. Two years earlier, Seafirst's total was $10 billion, and Rainier's $5.9 billion.

The quoted market price of Rainier's shares more than doubled, from a low of $17.375 in the third quarter of 1982 to an all-time high of $39.25 (before the 2-for-1 stock split in 1984) in the fourth quarter of 1983. According to *Marple's Business Newsletter*: "More basic to the rise in the stock is the growing realization among investors, including institutions, that Rainier has emerged as the

JUST ANOTHER DAY IN THE BANKING BIZ...

Local fears of interstate banking were captured humorously in this David Horsey cartoon, which ran in the Seattle Post-Intelligencer in 1983.

premier large banking organization in the Pacific Northwest."

Seafirst's fall reinforced Rainier Bancorporation's thinking about the balance between institutional and retail stock ownership. Corporate Treasurer Ronald H. Mead explained: "Up until the early '70s, most of the stock was held in our own backyard. The stock gradually expanded and had wider ownership as the company expanded its operations. Also, stock ownership from institutions started to pick up as we developed investor relations activities.

"We also recognized that the heart of this company was retail banking. And retail ownership was important to us. It helped reinforce our philosophy of keeping a balance between institutional and retail ownership, which we felt was important to a regional bank holding company. We generally kept the institutional ownership below 50 percent. That was reinforced when we saw what the institutional investors did to the stock of Seafirst when they had their problems."

The result of this good fortune was a record 1983, which followed a lackluster 1982. Net income in 1983—the first full year after interest rate ceilings came off most consumer deposits—increased 21 percent from 1982 to $47.2 million. More than 21 percent of net income was generated by Rainier Financial Services. As domestic loan demand waned, Rainier sought income from non-lending sources, such as consumer financial planning, leasing and other services.

At the annual meeting, the shareholders authorized a doubling of shares of common stock to 40 million, with 19.7 million outstanding. Truex cited a *Fortune* survey, covering the 10 years ended in 1982, that singled out Rainier as the best value among banks for shareholders, with an annual increase in share value and dividend payouts averaging about 13.5 percent.

Open Border Banking

With interstate banking on the horizon, Rainier was faced with three options: acquire smaller banks; merge with a bank of equal size, producing a super-regional bank that could compete with the big money-center banks; or be acquired by a large out-of-state bank. Future events would determine Rainier's ultimate direction.

But in the early 1980s, acquisitions were high on Rainier's agenda. Not since Andrew Price, Sr., had acquisitions been much of a factor in the bank's growth. The conservative Truex cautioned that Rainier was "not about to pay an outlandish price for anything. Instead of buying assets and market share, we have to think in terms of buying earnings and earnings potential. If we can do that on a reasonable basis, we'll do it."

In late October 1982, Rainier and Spokane-based Old National Bancorporation reached an agreement in principle to merge the two holding companies. Terms of the agreement called for the exchange of 0.925 share of Rainier common stock for each ONBC share. Old National had more than 2.4 million shares of common stock outstanding, but it was in financial trouble. By December, merger negotiations were terminated because the two bank holding companies were unable to reach mutually acceptable terms.

Two years later, ONBC signed a merger agreement with U.S. Bancorp of Portland, but the deal could not go through until Washington State passed a reciprocal interstate banking law; Oregon already had such a law.

Rainier became the focus of growing national and local speculation as a potential takeover target. In mid-1985, it was one of the few U.S. banks whose stock was selling for more than book value, and over the previous two years, its earnings had grown by more than 50 percent (30 percent in 1984). *Fortune* listed Rainier among seven banks "that security analysts said would make sound investments, whether or not they get caught up in the merger maelstrom."

Publicly and privately, Truex supported the tide toward interstate banking. He told the financial publication *Euromoney*: "The states are rolling over one by one, and we favor it."

Mangels focused the bank's interest: "Our criteria are not so much what we have to pay, but how much we earn on the investment."

Rainier began expanding its operation and customer base in preparation for interstate banking and to strengthen its position in the Washington market. With the announcement of a Lynnwood branch, Rainier became the first state bank to take advantage of Washington's 1985 intrastate banking law, which allowed banks to branch anywhere in the state. One of the primary goals of expansion was to achieve a "critical mass" of customers that would be large enough to spread the cost of development of new products, to deliver services with expensive sophisticated automated systems and to provide large corporate customers with a global network.

Despite all the talk of big out-of-state banks descending on Washington State, Rainier was not cutting back on expenditures and pumping up earnings in order to pretty itself up for a potential acquisition merger by an out-of-state bank. Instead, Rainier spent $90 million over a five-year period on new leading-edge electronic equipment

Overseeing the bank's substantial investment in the Tukwila operations center computer facilities in 1981 were Administrative Division Executive Vice President Richard W. Brandt (right) and Electronic Data Processing Vice President and Manager William Anderson.

and the facilities to sustain it.

Rainier was interested in acquisitions—but only on a prudent basis. An oft-quoted Truex remark of that period: "Our romance threshold is high so we don't do anything foolish."

In 1985 and 1986, Rainier completed seven mergers

and acquisitions, adding more than $1 billion in assets and almost 50 locations in western Washington, Alaska and Oregon. All deals involved tax-free exchanges of stock. Rainier Bancorporation's stock had been selling between 110 percent and 130 percent of book value, which meant that Rainier could acquire more with its stock without adversely depleting equity and diluting earnings.

The Oregon transaction, involving Mount Hood Security Bank in Gresham, was the first acquisition of an Oregon bank by a Washington bank, thanks to a new Oregon banking law that permitted the entrance of outside banks as of July 1, 1986.

Rainier looked to other parts of the West. In 1984, it explored merger with Bank of California, and in 1985, with Valley National Bank in Arizona, but neither effort bore fruit.

After two unsuccessful attempts to merge with Puget Sound Bancorp of Tacoma, which had 64 branches in the state and assets of $1.5 billion, Rainier had exhausted all reasonable acquisition possibilities—banks that would substantially increase Rainier's size.

Rainier's move into Oregon fueled speculation of a merger between Rainier and U.S. Bancorp of Portland, which was about the same size. The two medium-sized holding companies came close to joining forces, but after long negotiations and give-and-take on both sides, an agreement could not be reached. Among the major sticking points were personalities and style, and questions of who would lead the new organization, how many directors from each bank would serve on the board, and where the headquarters would be located. With the failure of the U.S. Bancorp merger, Rainier had exhausted one of its primary options.

"Once we decided we could never make a deal with U.S. Bank, then our options diminished," recalled Herman Sarkowsky, a Rainier director and Seattle investor and developer.

As for Rainier being acquired, Truex publicly insisted the chances were "slim. We would demand a pretty fancy price." But by 1986, more than half the states had enacted interstate banking laws in some form, and the industry was, in Truex's words, in the midst of a "feeding frenzy" as larger banks began buying smaller banks at record premiums. (Locally, U.S. Bancorp later merged its Washington holding company, Old National Bancorporation, with another U.S. Bancorp acquisition, Peoples Bancorporation; and KeyCorp. of Albany, New York, acquired Seattle Trust & Savings Bank.) Banks the size of Rainier were selling at an attractive 1986 average of 16.8 times annual earnings—about two times book value.

With size and accomplishment comes respect. Rainier Bank often hosted its directors and customers at meetings with national and international leaders in business and government. (From left) former United States President Gerald R. Ford, G. Robert Truex, Jr., and bank directors Lynn P. Himmelman and Herman Sarkowsky.

(From left)
John D. Mangels,
Jon M. Christoffersen and
G. Robert Truex, Jr.

In mid-1986, James C. Freund, a confidant of G. Robert Truex, Jr., and a partner in the New York law firm of Skadden, Arps, Slate, Meagher & Flom, joined Truex for dinner in Seattle. During their conversation, Truex expressed to Freund a logical argument for selling the bank. Truex felt that the timing was right. Banks were commanding high prices and a merger with a big bank would keep top management and middle management motivated. Truex, however, was reticent to make his position known to Rainier's board of directors.

Freund recalled: "He was concerned that the directors would think that the reason he wanted to sell the bank was that he wanted to cash in his chips, and that he would be remembered as the guy who came to Seattle from out of town and sold out the biggest independent bank in the state—for his own purposes.

"I said, 'But that's not the reason; you just gave me your reason… If you feel this is the right direction, you have to tell the directors and exert leadership.' "

The next night, Truex laid out his reasoning to the bank's executive committee and the following day to its full board of directors. He felt it wasn't the best course for Rainier to remain independent. "We're talking about the future of this company and the financial well-being of our shareholders," Truex said, "and that's what we have to concern ourselves with."

Director James A. Walsh, the retired president of Allied Stores, Inc., felt "we could sit still and let someone come out of the woods and take us over. Or we could look at whom we would like to join forces with. We wanted the

Rainier's 1985 board of directors (in ascending order): Orville E. Melby, John D. Mangels, G. Robert Truex, Jr., Wylie M. Hemphill, Marjorie W. Evans, Paul A. Redmond, Thomas H. O'Leary, James A. Walsh, Richard R. Albrecht, Francis G. Crane, Donald E. Schaake, C.M. Ambrose, Jr., Andrew Price, Jr., Louis Arrigoni, Herman Sarkowsky, Robert M. Helsell and Robert D. O'Brien. Not pictured: Nancy L. Jacob, C. Calvert Knudsen, Arne T. Lervick and Edward L. Palmer.

opportunity to look at the culture and philosophy of those institutions and have a hand in charting our own destiny."

Truex's speech to the board of directors started the ball rolling. Following the board's approval, Rainier hired Goldman Sachs & Co., the New York-based investment banking firm, to study what the bank was worth and to explore possible acquisition partners, specifically large institutions.

John Golden, a Goldman Sachs partner, recalled: "It was not a simple process to develop real interest in Rainier, which was a large transaction. It was not an easy bite for anyone."

Rainier was indeed a big bite. The corporation's assets included a network of 140 bank branches; relationships with more than 40 percent of the households in the second largest banking state west of Texas; a presence in Oregon and Alaska; and a system of Pacific Rim branches in Asia that was exceeded only by those of Citibank, Chase Manhattan and B of A.

After several months of exploration, the list of serious bidders came down to a pair: Security Pacific Corporation based in Los Angeles and First Bank System of Minneapolis. In the fall of 1986, both banks had purchased failing Washington State banks. First Bank acquired Mid-Valley Bank of Omak, renamed First Bank Washington; Security Pacific picked up Harbor Security Bank of McCleary and renamed it Washington Bank. (Security Pacific was initially interested in Mid-Valley.) These acquisitions were mere beachheads for future expansion in Washington under the state's new banking regulations.

Security Pacific Corporation and First Bank System were attracted by Rainier Bank's strategic Seattle base and that city's substantial international trade.

Both First Bank and Security Pacific were big enough to acquire Rainier. At the time, First Bank owned 78 banks and had 147 banking offices in Minnesota, Wisconsin, North and South Dakota, Idaho and Washington. The Pacific Northwest and the St. Louis area were its two principal targets.

Security Pacific Corporation, then the sixth largest bank holding company in the country, had assets in 1986 of $62.6 billion and a dozen years of bottom-line growth. Security Pacific had become a leader in developing non-interest sources of income, particularly from securities through investment banking services and the development of its own mutual funds.

Richard J. Flamson III, chairman of the board and chief executive officer of Security Pacific Corporation, wanted his company to have interstate banking account for 25 percent of profits by 1991. The remaining 75 percent would be divided among financial services, capital markets and California banking/retail operations.

Security Pacific's aims for an interstate banking network throughout the West were tied into its aggressive pursuit of Pacific Rim business. Robert H. Smith, president and chief executive officer of Security Pacific National Bank, explained: "We felt we could be closer geographically to one client base throughout the whole Pacific. We could have one customer link throughout the whole West Coast, which would give us greater economy and product availability to offer the clients of all the banking institutions."

In 1986, Security Pacific paid $460 million for Arizona Bancwest, owner of The Arizona Bank, that state's third largest bank, with assets of $4 billion; paid $52.5 million for Orbanco Financial Services, the third largest bank in Oregon, with assets of $1 billion; and signed a deal to buy The Nevada Bank, that state's largest, though the deal would not be final until Nevada's interstate banking law took effect on January 1, 1989.

Negotiations

Serious negotiations with both First Bank and Security Pacific took place in late 1986 and continued through early 1987 as Rainier directors met on several occasions with the principals of each bank, listened to their philosophies and questioned them about their direction.

The two rivals found themselves in a bidding war, and the price tag on Rainier began to rise. Finally, on February 23, 1987, the two bidders submitted their final proposals: Security Pacific offered stock then worth the equivalent of $52.33 a share; First Bank System, $52.80. Compared to the price of Rainier's stock in 1973 of $5.3125 (adjusted for stock splits in 1977 and 1984), the offers represented a handsome gain. The Rainier board met on the 40th floor of the Rainier Bank Tower to deliberate. Director Herman Sarkowsky described the discussions at the executive committee level as "hot and furious… There were some real knock-down, drag-out battles."

Rather than discuss matters before the board en masse, the Rainier board used discussion groups to expedite its business. Standing, (from left) John D. Mangels, Richard R. Albrecht, Arne T. Lervick, C. M. Ambrose, Jr., Donald E. Schaake, James A. Walsh, Louis Arrigoni, Orville E. Melby, Francis G. Crane and Herman Sarkowsky. Seated, (from left) W. J. Pennington, Wylie M. Hemphill, G. Robert Truex, Jr., Marjorie W. Evans and Andrew Price, Jr.

Most of Rainier's management and board were convinced that Security Pacific was a better fit for a variety of reasons. Corporate culture was an important consideration for Truex, who had a deep commitment to the future of the management team he had built over his 14 years with Rainier. (Indeed, the quality of that team added materially to the selling price of the bank.) Director C. Calvert Knudsen, vice chairman of MacMillan Bloedel Limited, felt "there was the same kind of culture in both organizations, something that provided not only a benefit for our customer base and our shareholders, but also a broader set of opportunities for our employees."

Sarkowsky agreed: "There wasn't any doubt that Security Pacific's offer was better from the standpoint of culture and a lot of other things." Nevertheless, "we, as directors, especially those of us on the executive committee, had to look at this in a different light. The cultures be damned. How much is culture worth if we can get a better return for our shareholders?"

Board member Richard R. Albrecht, executive vice president of Boeing Commercial Airplane Company, felt that Security Pacific was "a better fit from their Pacific Rim experience. We were bringing some strength to what Security Pacific already had in the Pacific Rim." On the other hand, "First Bank was looking for us to provide their international arm."

One of the many things Truex liked was the fact that Security Pacific represented a "powerful domestic banking company with a common orientation towards the consumer from Tijuana to Anchorage and across the Pacific."

During the directors' discussions, concern for how the merger would affect the local community was expressed by Andrew Price, Jr., who stood to gain financially as much as anyone. Board member Nancy L. Jacob, who was then dean of the University of Washington Schools of Business Administration, recalled: "Andrew gave a very carefully worded talk about his concerns, which we discussed for about an hour. I think most of the directors will credit Andrew with having raised that issue, so that we could deal with it. That's the kind of issue that you sometimes don't get involved in, only to regret it later."

On the evening of February 23, with one board member casting his vote by phone from a limousine in Manhattan, Rainier Bancorporation's board of directors accepted the bid of Security Pacific. The agreement called for an exchange of 1.3 shares of Security Pacific common stock for each Rainier share. Based on the $40.25-per-share closing price of Security Pacific stock on February 23, the value of the transaction to Rainier stockholders was approximately $1.15 billion, or $52.33 a share, which was 1.95 times Rainier's 1986 book value. It was the second largest friendly bank merger in history. And it was nearly three times the $400 million that B of A paid for Seafirst in 1983.

As part of the agreement, Truex and Knudsen were named to the Security Pacific board.

A delighted Security Pacific Chairman Flamson told *The Seattle Times* that Rainier "completes our strategy to be the dominant banking force in the West and on the Pacific Rim."

(From left) John D. Mangels, G. Robert Truex, Jr., and Security Pacific Corporation's president and chief operating officer, George F. Moody, announced the sale of Rainier Bancorporation to Security Pacific at a news conference on February 25, 1987.

Security Pacific Corporation Chairman Richard J. Flamson III.

Robert H. Smith, president and chief executive officer of Security Pacific National Bank.

Rainier stockholders received the equivalent of an annual rate of $1.92 per share, compared with Rainier's indicated annual dividend of $1.16, a 66-percent increase. Stockholders were also eligible for any increased dividends subsequently paid out by Security Pacific.

Security Pacific President Smith noted that Security Pacific entered the Rainier negotiations with a "fundamental philosophy that if we were going to pay that amount of money we didn't want to lose the franchise—Rainier's people and its presence in the market. You couldn't duplicate the value of that franchise; it was one of a kind. That's what makes you a more aggressive buyer. That's why we didn't pay any more than we thought we should, but they didn't leave much more on the table."

On Rainier Bank's side, the acquisition reached a successful conclusion because the system worked the way management and the board had designed it. The board members gave much of the credit to Truex. Albrecht called the process "orderly. Even if you look at the last 30 days, it might look like a very frenzied activity, but it was the culmination of a couple of years of preparation. We were ready."

Added to the equation of dividends, corporate cultures and multiple earnings was Truex's health. He suffered from advanced degenerative chronic emphysema. He was on a constant supply of oxygen and required the aid of a motorized cart to move much beyond the walls of his own office. Although others were concerned about his condition, Truex was not.

In one instance, in the middle of negotiations with

Flamson and Smith, an exhausted Truex had to lie down on the couch in his office. Flamson, who had previously expressed concern over Truex's health, said, "Bob, let's quit and call it off. It isn't worth it. The bottom line is your life. I'm not going to sit here and watch you kill yourself."

With a wave of his arm Truex dismissed their concern: "Don't worry about it. I'm just taking a rest."

Truex's objectives were clear, and he found within himself the strength to preside, assertively, over the most difficult, far-reaching decision in his years at Rainier Bank, and perhaps his entire professional life. And he did it, said Smith, with "great courage."

Freund called Truex's performance under pressure "brilliant and dramatic. These negotiations were very difficult. There were two parties in two different rooms, people were running back and forth, and here was Truex wheeling around in his cart conducting these meetings. I don't remember him missing a minute of the board meetings. He presented his own views forcefully but only after he let everybody speak his piece. It was a very classy performance."

It wasn't until after the merger had been approved by the boards of both Rainier and Security Pacific that Truex publicly brought out the issue of his health. At the conclusion of a long press conference in Seattle—in which he shared the stage with John D. Mangels and George F. Moody, chief operating officer of Security Pacific—Truex announced:

"People forever are passing around rumors about my health. In fact, there's a story in *The New York Times* wondering if this [merger] is being done because of my health. If you're of a mind to report, you can tell everybody—if you see what I think you see—that I chew nails and spit battleships, so don't worry about my health."

The Truex Legacy

On July 16, 1987, two days after Rainier Bancorporation stockholders approved the merger at the 60th annual stockholders meeting, Truex, 63, stepped down as chairman and chief executive officer and was replaced by Mangels, 61. "I've been chief executive officer for 14

Among many examples of his community involvement, G. Robert Truex , Jr., served as United Way's 1979-80 general campaign chairman.

years. It's just time," he told the *Seattle Post-Intelligencer*. He continued as chairman of the executive committee of the holding company and the bank, and as a director of both. Rainier Bank President Jon M. Christoffersen, 44, was named president of the holding company.

Of Mangels, Truex said, "My colleagues have heard me say often that I wouldn't want to come to work in the morning if John Mangels weren't here. That's hyperbole, but it makes the point. Most of the credit for the good stuff around here has come to me, whereas he deserves a very large measure—perhaps most—of it."

From the time Truex took the helm of Marine in 1973 until he stepped down as CEO, the market value of the corporation grew at an annual compound rate of 17.8 percent ($5.312 per share in 1973 to $52.625 at the time of the merger), compared with an average of 7.5 percent for the top 24 banks in the country, according to the Keefe Index. Rainier shareholders enjoyed a 21.8-percent total annual compound return—including stock price plus dividend—that was nearly double the average of the nation's 24 major banks.

Not surprisingly, when Truex was asked what his greatest satisfaction was, he said, "Taking a pretty stodgy, non-competitive enterprise, making it a factor in the market, and getting it to the point it gets national recognition."

When the final figures on the merger were reached on August 31, 1987, Security Pacific's stock price closed at $42.375 a share, making Rainier's value $55.0875 a share, which was more than $2.50 higher than when the deal was

Known as much for his humor as his intellect, G. Robert Truex, Jr., showed his sense of whimsy with this welcome mat outside his office door.

announced in February. Rainier's 5,800 shareholders became owners of Security Pacific stock worth $1.22 billion. And their dividends doubled.

Truex Touched Every Aspect of Rainier Bank

Productivity improved through increased use of electronic technology and automated systems. In 1981, Rainier co-founded a nationwide network of more than 5,000 automated teller machines. The reciprocal arrangement allowed all members access to ATMs of member banks. In 1985, PeoplesBank and Rainier Bank opened 152 bank machines in Safeway supermarkets and grocery stores

affiliated with Associated Grocers. That same year, Rainier installed a bank machine at Hewlett-Packard's instrument factory at Lake Stevens—the first in Washington at a place of work other than a bank.

John D. Mangels was elected
chairman of the board of both
Rainier Bank and Rainier
Bancorporation in July 1987.

(Left) The Mt. St. Helens eruption of 1980.

(Center) Washington and Alaska salmon fishing.

(Right) Washington and Alaska forest products.

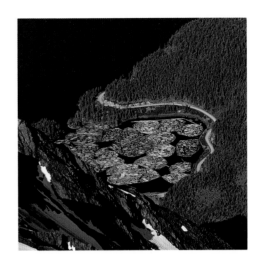

Under Truex, Rainier Bank continued and enhanced its support of the Northwest's primary industries, aerospace, agriculture, forest products, fishing and international trade, which were notoriously cyclical in nature. At the 1984 annual meeting, Truex told shareholders that "I don't mind having trouble with a local industry. They'll ride it out and survive. It is important for banks to back their major local industries in times of stress."

For example, in 1980, when farmers were hit by changing economic conditions, mounting energy and interest costs, and the damaging effects of the Mt. St. Helens volcanic eruption, the bank came to the rescue. Rainier slashed its interest rates from as high as 21 percent to 14 percent on current agricultural loans of more than $25,000, and reinstated a discontinued VISA Bank Line program for customers to borrow money for major purchases, including repairs on automobiles and equipment.

Agriculture—primarily grain, wheat, cattle and

apples, and food processing—annually accounted for approximately $300 million in loans, about 7 percent of the bank's total portfolio. Rainier was one of the few banks in the country that carried a separate total for agriculture loans outside the commercial loan portfolio. Prior to the merger, Rainier was the nation's fifth largest agricultural lender. Combined with Security Pacific's $540 million in farm loans, the two banks together became the second largest agri-lender in the country.

In fishing, Rainier financed about 50 percent of the U.S. salmon-packing industry and became a factor for the industry on both the East and West coasts of the United States. Rainier financed the boats, the catches and the processing of the seafood, including salmon, halibut, bottom fish, crab and shrimp.

Rainier was one of only two banks in the country with a specialized Forest Products Group, and developed a national and international reputation lending to the industry, from Northern California redwoods through the Northwest and up to Alaska spruce.

Community Involvement

Rainier's policy was praised in the publication *Insight: The Advisory Letter for Concerned Investors*, which said in 1984: "With the exception of South Shore Bank in Chicago, we are not aware of any other bank of this size that has so completely integrated social and business concerns in the structure of their organization. Social performance has been made part of the company's day-to-day business."

One of the point men in this effort was Mangels, who was active in many civic and charitable organizations, including United Way of King County, for which he served as chairman. "If you want to be successful in this organization, you have to get involved in the community," Mangels had noted. "Our corporate prosperity is a direct function of the prosperity of the community."

Rainier Community Service Corporation made

short-term loans on projects until long-term financing could be arranged. The Rainier Home Loan Center helped the Seattle Housing Resources Group find affordable properties for low-income housing uses. In 1985, the center donated property and a duplex, which later was renovated for use as interim crisis housing.

In the Rainier Bank tradition of public service, John D. Mangels served United Way as its 1985 chairman.

In 1985, Rainier's Cash Management Consulting Group developed overnight investment services for the Yakima Nation. The Indian nation's leaders had been working to increase returns from its timber harvest and support industries in order to create jobs and improve the social and health services for the more than 7,000 tribal members. Marjorie W. Evans, a bank director recruited by Truex, saw the tribe as an important social and business opportunity for the bank.

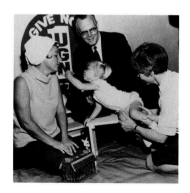

(From left) Maxwell Carlson received the chairman's United Good Neighbor (United Way) gavel from its outgoing chairman, Seattle Times publisher and NB of C director W.J. Pennington. T. Robert Faragher served as United Way chairman in 1970. Also active in United Way, Andrew Price, Jr., took various leadership roles with the Boy Scouts of America. In 1986, G. Robert Truex, Jr., received the Fourth Annual Breath of Life Award from the Patrons of Cystic Fibrosis for his work with that organization.

Evans also encouraged the bank's involvement with women and minorities, both as customers and employees. In 1985, the bank opened its Community Business Loan Center to meet the capital servicing needs of small-business owners, particularly minorities and women. By 1988, the center had a portfolio worth almost $5 million. Of the 60 loans outstanding, half were to businesses owned by women, such as retail stores, restaurants and construction firms.

In 1983, Rainier Bank was named in *The 100 Best Companies to Work for in America.* One of the other banks included in the list was Security Pacific. George F. Moody, chief operating officer of Security Pacific Corporation, described his bank as having "some of the best employee programs in the country. We have a volunteer program: 4,200 of our employees and retirees contributed over 40,000 hours of community service last year. Our foundation gave $5 million away. In 1986, President Reagan identified Security Pacific as the leading corporation in community involvement and volunteerism."

On August 24, 1988, Truex died following a brief final battle with emphysema. A *Seattle Times* editorial praised Truex as a community leader, particularly for his work with the Washington Roundtable, which Truex helped found: "...Truex helped to bring together two factions that historically viewed each other with suspicion—business leaders and politicians—forging new ideas for education and other programs at the state level. Because he was a role model, Truex leaves a living legacy on the Pacific coast, a thriving sensitivity in the corporate

world to the daily well-being of all its neighbors."

Changes Under Security Pacific

"One of the great lies in America, along with 'the check is in the mail,' is that 'everything will be the same after the merger.' It can't be the same. There are going to be substantial changes," Mangels told a May 1987 banking industry conference in Coeur d'Alene, Idaho.

Beginning in November 1987, Rainier began to shed about $1.5 billion of its $9.5 billion in assets—including the mortgage and leasing companies, which duplicated existing Security Pacific operations.

When the acquisition became final, Rainier's international operations merged into Security Pacific's and duplicate branches were either sold or closed.

While Rainier lost those assets, the Oregon Bank, with $1.2 billion in assets and 56 offices, came under Rainier management. That move was part of a direction to refocus assets and energies on the Pacific Northwest.

Rainier's creative management was encouraged by its parent. In the spring of 1988, Rainier opened a "retail investment center" on the mezzanine level of the Rainier Bank Tower. The first of its kind in a Seattle commercial bank, the center was staffed by personal financial planners, discount brokers and trust officers. At the same time, Rainier announced plans for small branch bank operations in Safeway supermarkets throughout Washington.

Along with the reality of change, Security Pacific brought to Rainier Bank new products beyond the scope of any $9 billion bank. In addition to state-of-the-art technology, Security Pacific offered Rainier customers the resources of a $72 billion asset base—far more than the combined assets of Washington State banks.

Rainier availed itself of Security Pacific's merchant banking capabilities, which helped Pacific Northwest businesses raise money directly in the securities market instead of borrowing it from banks. Flamson noted: "There is a need to develop worldwide capacity in every money center around the world. In this way, positions in foreign exchange or equities or debt instruments can be efficiently passed around the world."

After the merger, Rainier was able to provide key customers access to capital markets. In December 1987, for example, Rainier structured for Longview Fibre a $95 million competitive bid financing. This Security Pacific merchant banking product allowed its New York corpo-

George F. Moody, president and chief operating officer of Security Pacific Corporation, was elected to the board of Rainier Bancorporation following the merger in 1987.

rate debt desk to sell Longview Fibre short-term loans.

Changes in personnel were minimal, perhaps one reason being Moody's own sensitivity to the situation: "I was the result of an acquisition when the then-Security First National Bank bought Citizen's National Bank. I know what being acquired is like."

Security Pacific waited until the summer of 1988 before naming John C. Getzelman, one of its own executives, president and chief operating officer of Rainier Bancorporation and Rainier Bank, and chairman of the Oregon Bank. He replaced Jon M. Christoffersen, who became president of VISA U.S.A., Inc. Getzelman, 45, had

Following its acquisition by Security Pacific, Rainier ventured into new capital services. In 1987, it served as a merchant bank for the sale of short-term loans for Longview Fibre.

Security Pacific Bank Washington vice chairmen: (From left) Gordon F. Givens, David I. Williams, Stanley D. Savage and W. Thomas Porter, Jr.

joined Security Pacific in 1971 and became executive vice president in 1984. He was formerly managing director of Security Pacific's International Merchant Bank.

In late 1988, two weeks following the announcement that Security Pacific's Arizona bank name would change to Security Pacific Bank Arizona, the Rainier Bancorporation board voted to change the name of Rainier Bank to Security Pacific Bank Washington. Name changes for Security Pacific's Alaska, Oregon and Nevada banks were also approved by their boards.

Mangels said, "We have considerable equity in the Rainier name, and we change it only after careful deliberation. However, the advantages of a common identity throughout the Security Pacific family provide a powerful argument for making the change…"

Knowing the history of Rainier's name change from National Bank of Commerce of Seattle in 1974, the Corporate Communications Department manned a phone bank to handle what was expected to be an outcry from those customers who felt disenfranchised. The calls never came.

Such changes aroused some concern in Washington State about the bank's future direction. It was Mangels who lent new perspective to the matter. In an interview with the *Seattle Weekly*, Mangels was asked whether Security Pacific had grand plans for its Seattle subsidiary. His response: "We… have grand plans for ourselves."

John D. Mangels (left), chairman, and John C. Getzelman, president, Security Pacific Bank Washington, with portraits of prior leaders Maxwell Carlson (left), and Andrew Price.

Books and Monographs:

Clark, Norman H., *Washington: A Bicentennial History*. W.W. Norton & Company, Inc.: New York, 1976.

Compton, Eric N., *Principles of Banking*. Second Edition. American Bankers Association:Washington, D.C., 1983.

Dorpat, Paul, *Seattle Now & Then*. Tartu Publications: Seattle, 1984.

Dunbar, Charles F., Willis, Henry Parker, and Sprague, Oliver M.W., *The Theory and History of Banking*. Fifth Edition, G.P. Putnam's Sons: New York, 1929.

Federal Reserve, Board of Governors, *The Federal Reserve System, Purposes and Functions*. The Federal Reserve: Washington, D.C., 1974.

James, Marquis, and James, Bessie R., *Biography of a Bank, the Story of the Bank of America*. Harper & Brothers: New York, 1954.

Marple, Elliot, and Olson, Bruce H., *The National Bank of Commerce of Seattle, 1889-1969*. Pacific Books: Palo Alto, 1970.

Morgan, Murray, *Skid Road*. The Viking Press: New York, 1951.

Moskowitz, Milton, *The 100 Best Companies to Work for in America*. Addison-Wesley Publishing Company: Redding, MA, 1984

Provorse, Barry L., *The PeoplesBank Story*. Documentary Book Publishers Corporation: Bellevue, WA, 1987.

Sales, Roger, *Seattle Past to Present*. University of Washington Press: Seattle, 1976.

Scates, Shelby, *FIRSTBANK The Story of Seattle-First National Bank*. Seattle-First National Bank: Seattle, 1970.

Speidel, William C., *Sons of the Profits*. Nettle Creek Publishing Company: Seattle, 1967.

Zweig, Phillip L., *Belly Up: The Collapse of the Penn Square Bank*. Crown Publishers, Inc.: New York, 1985.

Trade Periodicals, Business Publications and Newspapers:

ABA Banking Journal
Adweek
American Banker
Anchorage Daily News
Bellevue Journal-American
Burroughs Clearing House
Business Month
BusinessWeek

California Business
Daily Journal of Commerce
Daily Olympian
Euromoney
Federal Banking Law Reports
Federal Register
Financial World
Forbes
Fortune
Everett Herald
Insight: The Advisory Letter for Concerned Investors
Institutional Investor
Marple's Business Newsletter
Montesano Vidette
NB of C News
National Bank of Commerce Meridians
News From Marine Bancorporation
Newsweek
Pacific Banker
Pacific Northwest Executive
Pensions & Investment Age
Piper, Jaffray & Hopwood Executive Summary
Poulsbo/Kitsap County Herald
Puget Sound Business Journal
Rainier Bancorporation Bulletin
Rainier Bank Echo
Rainier Bank Venture
Rainier Bancorporation: The Pacific Northwest Economy, 1984, 1985
Rainier Bancorporation Social Performance Journal
Rainier Bancorporation Manager
Rainier Economic Perspective
Seattle Argus

Seattle Daily Journal of Commerce
Seattle Weekly
Security Pacific: The Story of a Bank
Security News
Sedro-Woolley Courier-Times
Spokane Daily-Chronicle
Tacoma News Tribune
The Bankers Magazine
The New York Times
The Oregonian
Seattle Post-Intelligencer
The Seattle Times
The Shrewsbury, N.J. Register
The Wall Street Journal
United States Banker
Vancouver Columbian
Washington Financial Reports
Waterville Empire-Press
Wenatchee Daily World
Western Banker
Yakima Herald-Republic

Annual Reports:

Marine Bancorporation and National Bank
of Commerce of Seattle, 1965-1973
Rainier Bancorporation: 1974-1987
Security Pacific Corporation: 1986 and
1987

Correspondence, Notes, Memoranda:

Carlson, Maxwell
Faragher, T. Robert
Marple, Elliot
National Bank of Commerce of Seattle
Rainier Bancorporation

Elliot Marple Notes:

Walter J. Funk
Edgar A. Ruth
Mrs. Merle Johnson Harp
Dale Courtney
David H. Scott
E. Carter Shannon
Ralph J. Stowell
J.A. Swalwell
George W. Waller
Ross P. Williams

Transcribed Oral History Interviews with Current and Retired National Bank of Commerce, Rainier Bank and Security Pacific Corporation Executives:

Earnest E. Baker*
Robert F. Buck
Maxwell Carlson*
C. R. Chadwick
Jon M. Christoffersen
Kenneth J. Clark*
John F. Cockburn
Michael J. Coie
James D. Cullen
Robert C. Cummings
T. Robert Faragher
Harold O. Fenno
Richard J. Flamson III
Gordon F. Givens
John F. Hall*
Jack Horn
Clarence L. Hulford
Robert M. Ingram III
Sarah M.R. (Sally) Jewell
James C. Kearney
Bruce A. Koppe
Wilbur H. McGuire
Chester C. Macneill
John D. Mangels
Robert H. Matthews
Ronald H. Mead
Orville E. Melby
George F. Moody
Lenore Petrick*

W. Thomas Porter, Jr.
Andrew Price, Jr.
Maurice J. Santi
Stanley D. Savage
Robert H. Smith
Ralph J. Stowell
Donald B. Summers
Robert J. Svare
John M. Teutsch, Jr.*
G. Robert Truex, Jr.
William J. Waldo
David I. Williams

Directors:

Richard R. Albrecht
Louis Arrigoni
Prentice Bloedel*
Winston D. Brown
Bryant R. Dunn
Marjorie W. Evans
Stanley D. Golub
Wylie M. Hemphill
Nancy L. Jacob
C. Calvert Knudsen
Robert D. O'Brien
Thomas H. O'Leary
Herman Sarkowsky
James A. Walsh

*History Associates 1986 interviews.

Outside Experts:

Harry L. Coderre
James C. Freund
John Golden
Elliot Marple
Michael J. Parks
Brooks Ragen

Photography Credits:

All photographs not credited below are part of Security Pacific Bank Washington's archive.

Cover   Nick Gunderson/West Stock
Page II   Nick Gunderson/West Stock
Page VIII, Left, Rex Rystad
Page VIII, Right, Rex Rystad
Page 35 Dolph Zubick
Page 37 The Boeing Company
Page 56 The Seattle Times/Vic Condiotty
Page 59 Wallace Ackerman
Page 61 Bill Cannon
Page 62 Seattle Seahawks
Page 66 The Seattle Times/Ron De Rosa
Page 69 Walter Hodges
Page 72 Rex Rystad
Page 73 Frank Denman
Page 74 Walter Hodges
Page 81 Walter Hodges
Page 83 Seattle Post-Intelligencer/David Horsey
Page 85 Walter Hodges
Page 88 The Seattle Times

Page 89 David Perry
Page 90 Louis Bencze
Page 91 Bill Cannon
Page 93 The Seattle Times
Page 95 United Way
Page 96 Rex Rystad
Page 98 Center, Barry Provorse
Page 98 Right, Barry Provorse
Page 99 From left:
        The Seattle Times
        The Seattle Times
        Forde Photography
        Wallace Ackerman
Page 101 Bottom, Frank Denman
Page 102 Rex Rystad
Page 103 Rex Rystad

Index

A

Aberdeen, WA, 10, 17
Administrative Division, 52
Affirmative Lending Program, 65
agriculture, 2, 3, 5, 13, 24, 29, 77, 98
Alaska Airlines, 61
Alaska, 3, 24, 98
Alaska Division, 52
Albrecht, Richard R., 89 (illus.), 91 (illus.), 92, 94
Alien banking law, 25
Almira branch, 27 (illus.)
Aloha Airlines, 61
aluminum industry, 13, 27
Ambrose, C. M., Jr., 64 (illus.), 89 (illus.), 91 (illus.)
American Banker quoted, 50, 51, 53, 70, 75
American Express, 75
Anatomy of an Airline, a History of National Airlines, The, 45
Anderson, Jeffrey, 78, 80-81
Anderson, William, 85 (illus.)
Arizona Bancwest, 91
Arizona Bank, The, 91
Arnold, M. A., 10-11, 17
Arrigoni, Louis, 43, 64 (illus.), 89 (illus.), 91 (illus.)
Asset and Liability Management, 49, 51, 63
Associated Grocers, 96
automated teller machines, 96

B

Bache Securities, 75
Backus, Manson F., 4, 5 (illus.), 6, 7 (illus.), 10-13, 21, 30
Bancitaly Corp., 10
bancorporation, 10
Bank Holding Company Act, 33, 76
Bank of America, 24, 33, 43, 45-47, 50, 51, 65, 69, 75, 77, 81-82, 90, 92
Bank of California, 36, 46, 86
Bank of Commerce, 2-4
Bank of Elma, 11
Bank of Everett, 77
BankAmericard, 32, 33 (illus.), 36, 48 (see

VISA)
Bedle, Ira W., 15
Bellevue branch, 27
Bellingham branch, 30
Belly Up, 81
Bishop, E. K., 5
Bloedel, Prentice, 42 (illus.) 43
Blyth Eastman Dillon & Co., 58
Boeing Company, The, 13, 24, 26, 33, 37 (illus.), 38, 46, 52, 61, 77
Bolger, Thomas E., 36
Bonneville power project, 13
Boyd, Homer L., 15, 19
branch banking, 9, 13-14, 21, 25, 27, 47, 50
Brandt, Richard W., 85 (illus.)
Brown, Winston D., 43, 64 (illus.)
Buck, Robert F., 28, 29 (illus.), 54, 61, 66, 67
Bunn, Wallace R., 64 (illus.)
Burlington branch, 29
Business Week quoted, 70, 72, 76-77

C

California Business quoted, 65
Campbell Soup, 61
Capital National Bank of Olympia, 10 (illus.)
Carlson, Gust A., 17
Carlson, Maxwell, 10, 15, 16 (illus.), 17, 18 (illus.), 19-21, 22 (illus.), 23-24, 25 (illus.), 27-28, 29 (illus.), 30-31, 32 (illus.), 33, 35-36, 39-40, 42 (illus.), 43, 45, 47, 50, 52, 58, 59 (illus.), 67, 71, 99 (illus.), 103 (illus.)
Carrington, Glen, 42 (illus.)
Carter administration, 75
Cash Management Consulting Group, 99
Century Plaza Hotel, 67
Central branch, 36
Chadwick, C. R., 72 (illus.)
Charles Schwab & Co., 75
Chase Manhattan, 52, 78, 90
Christoffersen, Jon M., 88 (illus.), 96, 101
Citibank, 33, 77, 90
Citizen's National Bank, 101
Citizens State Bank of Puyallup, 48
Clark, Norman, H., 1, 3
Clausen, A. W. (Tom), 43, 46
Clift, Walter, 22 (illus.)
Coast Mortgage Company, 34-35, 47, 53
Cockburn, John F., 52 (illus.), 78

Coderre, Dr. Harry, 50-51
Coie, Michael J., 71
Coldwell Banker, 75
Commerce House, 46
Commencement Bay, 1
Commerce Credit Company, 53
Community Business Loan Center, 100
Consumer Home Improvement Loan Department, 14
Continental Airlines, 52
Continental Illinois Bank and Trust, 78, 81
Corporate Banking Group, 52, 70
Corporate Communications Department, 102
Crane, Francis G., 64 (illus.), 89 (illus.), 91 (illus.)
Cummings, Robert C., 32, 33 (illus.)
Cystic Fibrosis, 99 (illus.)

D

Darigold, 24
Davies, Griffith, 2
Dean Witter Reynolds, 75
Delorie, Louie, 23
Depression, 11, 13, 19, 20, 23
deregulation, 75, 77
Dexter Horton & Company, 1-2
Dexter Horton Bank, 2, 9, 11
Dexter Horton estate, 5
Dunn, Bryant, 64 (illus.)

E

Eastman, Dean H., 42 (illus.)
Edge Act, 24, 25, 76
Energy-Lending Group, 78
Eurodollars, 24
Euromoney quoted, 85
Evans, Marjorie W., 64 (illus.), 65 (illus.), 89 (illus.), 91 (illus.), 99

F

Faragher, Arthur W., 15, 18 (illus.), 36, 42 (illus.)
Faragher, T. Robert (Bob), 33, 35 (illus.), 35-37, 38 (illus.), 39-40, 41 (illus.), 42 (illus.), 43, 47, 48, 51, 55-56, 64 (illus.), 66-67, 71 (illus.), 99 (illus.)
Federal Deposit Insurance Corporation (FDIC), 13, 81